HOUGHTON MIFFLIN HARCOURT

WRITE SOURCE

MW00805947

Daily Language Workouts

Grade 6

Interactive Whiteboard Compatible!

Daily MUG Shot Sentences

Weekly MUG Shot Paragraphs

Writing Prompts

Writing Topics

Show-Me Sentences

GREAT SOURCE.

 HOUGHTON MIFFLIN HARCOURT

A Few Words About
Daily Language Workouts Grade 6

Before you begin . . .

The activities in this book will help your students develop basic writing and language skills. You'll find three types of exercises on the following pages:

MUG Shot Sentences There are 175 sentences highlighting **m**echanics, **u**sage, and/or **g**rammar (MUG). That's one for each day of the school year, arranged in 35 weekly groups. Students correct the errors included in each sentence, developing both writing and editing skills in the process.

MUG Shot Paragraphs There are 35 weekly paragraphs. Each paragraph covers many of the same skills as the five daily sentences and serves as a concise review of the week's activities.

Daily Writing Practice This section begins with **writing prompts** that include topics and graphics designed to inspire expository, narrative, descriptive, persuasive, and creative writing. Next, a discussion of daily journal writing introduces the lists of intriguing **writing topics**. Finally, the **show-me sentences** provide starting points for paragraphs, essays, and other writing forms.

Write Source Online provides the lessons in this book for interactive whiteboard instruction. To use, open the files from *Write Source Online* using your whiteboard software.

Photo Acknowledgments   Cover (solar panels) ©Digital Vision/Getty Images; cover (astronaut) 116, 122, 136 ©Corbis; cover (moon) NASA; cover (windows), cover (Saturn and star), 124 132, 135, 138, 146 (goggles) ©Photodisc/Getty Images; cover (headset), 146 (fish, microphone) ©Comstock/Getty Images 117 ©Colin Anderson/Brand X/Corbis; 118 ©Stocktrek/Brand X/Getty Images; 125 HMH Collection; 126 ©Image Club/Getty Images; 129 ©Geo Images/Alamy.

Printed in the U.S.A.

ISBN   978-0-547-48517-1

2 3 4 5 6 7 8 9 10 11 12 0956 15 14 13 12 11

4500295808   A B C D E F G

Table of Contents

Editing and Proofreading Marks

Use these symbols to correct each MUG Shot sentence and paragraph.

Insert here.

∧

them
take∧home

Insert a comma, a semicolon, or a colon.

∧, ∧; ∧:

Troy∧,Michigan

Insert (add) a period.

⊙

Mrs⊙

Insert a hyphen or a dash.

⁻∧ ‾∧

one∧⁻third cup

Insert a question mark or an exclamation point.

?∧ !∧

How about you∧?

Capitalize a letter.

/ (or) ≡

T
/toronto (or) toronto
≡

Make a capital letter lowercase.

/

h
/History

Replace or delete (take out).

— (or) ⌐⌐

cold   *hot*
a ~~hot~~ day (or) a ~~not~~ day
(or) a ~~hot~~ day

Insert an apostrophe or quotation marks.

∨' ∨" ∨"

∨'   ∨"   ∨"
Bill's   "Wow!"

Use italics.

_____

Tracker

Insert parentheses.

(∧)∧

letters(∧from A to Z)∧

improve
punctuate

MUG Shot Sentences

The MUG Shot sentences are designed to be used at the beginning of each class period as a quick and efficient way to review **m**echanics, **u**sage, and **g**rammar. Each sentence can be corrected and discussed in 3 to 5 minutes.

SPELL edit
capitalize

MUG Shot Sentence Organizer

Original Sentence:

_____

_____

Corrected Sentence:

_____

_____

Original Sentence:

_____

_____

Corrected Sentence:

_____

_____

Original Sentence:

_____

_____

Corrected Sentence:

_____

_____

Original Sentence:

_____

_____

Corrected Sentence:

_____

_____

Original Sentence:

_____

_____

Corrected Sentence:

_____

Implementation and Evaluation

There are 35 weeks of daily MUG Shot sentences. The students may use the "Editing and Proofreading Marks" in *Write Source* or on page iv of this book to make corrections.

Implementation

On the days that you use MUG Shot sentences, we suggest that you write one or two of them on the board at the beginning of the class period. Allow students time to read each sentence to themselves. (Make sure they understand the sentences.) Then have students correct each MUG Shot in a space reserved for them in their notebooks (or on a copy of the "MUG Shot Sentence Organizer" provided on page 2 of this book). Next, have students discuss their corrections in pairs or as a class. Make sure everyone records the corrections on their papers. And, more importantly, make sure all students understand why the corrections were made.

You may also have students correct the sentences orally. Write the corrections on the board as students provide them. (Use the proofreading marks on page iv.) Have one student explain his or her corrections and discuss the results. Then ask all students to write the corrected form in their notebooks.

Each Friday, review the MUG Shots covered for the week. You might assign the MUG Shot paragraph that contains errors similar to the type students have worked on for the week. (See page 75.)

Note: By design, each page of sentences can be reproduced for student use or made into an overhead transparency.

Evaluation

If you assign sentences daily, evaluate your students' work at the end of each week. We recommend that you give them a basic performance score for their daily work. This performance score might be based on having each sentence for that week correctly written in their language arts notebooks (before or after any discussion).

You can also use the weekly paragraphs to evaluate student progress. The paragraphs cover the same kinds of errors as the sentences, so students should be able to cover a good percentage of these errors.

WEEK 1: Did You Know?

■ **Using the Right Word, Subject-Verb Agreement, Apostrophe (Possessives)**

A sneeze are you're bodys weigh of getting rid of irritants.

■ **Using the Right Word, Apostrophe, End Punctuation**

Did you no that its impossible to sneeze and keep your eyes open

at the same time

■ **Plurals, Quotation Marks, Comma (Dialogue)**

There are about 50 bones in a pair of human foots the doctor explained.

■ **Using the Right Word, Numbers, Adjective (Articles)**

An human heart beets about one hundred thousand times a day.

■ **Apostrophe, Comma (To Separate Phrases and Clauses), Spelling, Using the Right Word**

If astronauts dont excercise in space weightlessness eventually causes

there muscles to shrink.

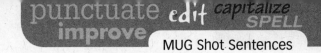

WEEK 1: Corrected Sentences

■ **Using the Right Word, Subject-Verb Agreement, Apostrophe (Possessives)**

A sneeze ~~are~~ *is* ~~you're~~ *your* body's ~~weigh~~ *way* of getting rid of irritants.

■ **Using the Right Word, Apostrophe, End Punctuation**

Did you ~~no~~ *know* that it's impossible to sneeze and keep your eyes open

at the same time *?*

■ **Plurals, Quotation Marks, Comma (Dialogue)**

"There are about 50 bones in a pair of human ~~foots~~ *feet*," the doctor explained.

■ **Using the Right Word, Numbers, Adjective (Articles)**

~~An~~ *A* human heart ~~beets~~ *beats* about ~~one hundred thousand~~ *100,000* times a day.

■ **Apostrophe, Comma (To Separate Phrases and Clauses), Spelling, Using the Right Word**

If astronauts don't ~~excercise~~ *exercise* in space, weightlessness eventually causes

~~there~~ *their* muscles to shrink.

WEEK 2: More Science Facts

■ **Using the Right Word, Apostrophe**

Accept for the fact that it can be burned, its almost impossible to destroy human hare.

■ **Apostrophe, Using the Right Word, Capitalization, Comma (Interruptions)**

A person living at the North pole in Winter wouldnt catch a cold amazingly because its to cold for germs to live there.

■ **Abbreviations, Comma (Interjections), Numbers**

Wow about seventy % of the earth is covered with H_2O.

■ **Using the Right Word, Comma (To Separate Adjectives), Spelling**

When you eat a peace of fresh crunchy celery, you burn more caleries then the celery contains.

■ **Capitalization, Adverb (Comparative/Superlative), Apostrophe (Possessives)**

A Womans heart beats more faster than a Mans.

WEEK 2: Corrected Sentences

■ **Using the Right Word, Apostrophe**

Except
~~Accept~~ for the fact that it can be burned, it's almost impossible to destroy

hair
human ~~hare~~.

■ **Apostrophe, Using the Right Word, Capitalization, Comma (Interruptions)**

A person living at the North *P*ole in *W*inter wouldn't catch a cold,

too
amazingly, because it's ~~to~~ cold for germs to live there.

■ **Abbreviations, Comma (Interjections), Numbers**

70 percent   *water*
Wow, about ~~seventy~~ % of the earth is covered with ~~H₂0~~.

■ **Using the Right Word, Comma (To Separate Adjectives), Spelling**

piece   *calories*
When you eat a ~~peace~~ of fresh, crunchy celery, you burn more ~~caleries~~

than
~~then~~ the celery contains.

■ **Capitalization, Adverb (Comparative/Superlative), Apostrophe (Possessives)**

A *W*oman's heart beats ~~more~~ faster than a *M*an's.

WEEK 3: Physical Science

■ **Using the Right Word, Subject-Verb Agreement, Parentheses**

Taste buds can't taste anything if their dry they requires saliva

to work).

■ **Apostrophe (Possessives), Pronoun-Antecedent Agreement, End Punctuation**

Would you believe that a persons tongue print is as unique as their

fingerprints

■ **Adverb (Comparative/Superlative), Subject-Verb Agreement**

Clouds flies more higher during the day than during the night.

■ **Comma (Series and To Separate Phrases and Clauses)**

In general girls learn to talk create sentences and read sooner than boys.

■ **Subject-Verb Agreement, Apostrophe, Using the Right Word**

People which smoke gets 65 percent more colds than people who dont

smoke.

WEEK 3: Corrected Sentences

■ **Using the Right Word, Subject-Verb Agreement, Parentheses**

Taste buds can't taste anything if ~~their~~ *they're* dry (they ~~requires~~ *require* saliva

to work).

■ **Apostrophe (Possessives), Pronoun-Antecedent Agreement, End Punctuation**

Would you believe that a person's tongue print is as unique as ~~their~~ *his or her*

fingerprints ?

■ **Adverb (Comparative/Superlative), Subject-Verb Agreement**

Clouds ~~flies~~ *fly* ~~more~~ higher during the day than during the night.

■ **Comma (Series and To Separate Phrases and Clauses)**

In general, girls learn to talk, create sentences, and read sooner than boys.

■ **Subject-Verb Agreement, Apostrophe, Using the Right Word**

People ~~which~~ *who* smoke ~~gets~~ *get* 65 percent more colds than people who don't

smoke.

WEEK 4: Believe It or Not

■ **Parallelism, Apostrophe, Comma (Interjections), End Punctuation**

Well I bet you cant breathe, chew, and be swallowing at the same time

■ **Using the Right Word, Comma (To Separate Phrases and Clauses)**

If your right-handed your fingernails grow faster on you're right hand.

■ **Pronoun-Antecedent Agreement, Capitalization, Rambling Sentence**

My Aunt told me that eyebrows will grow back if you pluck them, but not if you shave it off and I don't believe that because my friend shaved hers and it grew back.

■ **Semicolon, Double Negative**

A peanut isn't no nut, it's a bean.

■ **Subject-Verb Agreement, Using the Right Word, End Punctuation**

Did you no that plants breathes out the oxygen we need too breathe in

WEEK 4: Corrected Sentences

■ **Parallelism, Apostrophe, Comma (Interjections), End Punctuation**

Well, I bet you can't breathe, chew, and ~~be swallowing~~ *swallow* at the same time! *(or)* ⊙

■ **Using the Right Word, Comma (To Separate Phrases and Clauses)**

If *you're* ~~your~~ right-handed, your fingernails grow faster on *your* ~~you're~~ right hand.

■ **Pronoun-Antecedent Agreement, Capitalization, Rambling Sentence**

My *a* ~~A~~unt told me that eyebrows will grow back if you pluck them, but

not if you shave ~~it~~ *them* off. ~~and~~ I don't believe that because my friend shaved

hers and ~~it~~ *they* grew back.

■ **Semicolon, Double Negative**

A peanut isn't ~~no~~ *a* nut; it's a bean.

■ **Subject-Verb Agreement, Using the Right Word, End Punctuation**

Did you ~~no~~ *know* that plants ~~breathes~~ *breathe* out the oxygen we need ~~too~~ *to* breathe in?

WEEK 5: Parachutes to Planets

■ **Comma (Series and Unnecessary), Using the Right Word**

The parachute was used in 1783 to save people, whom had to jump from burning buildings high towers and other dangerous places.

■ **Using the Right Word, Numbers, Spelling**

Earth moves threw space 8 times faster than a speeding bullit.

■ **Using the Right Word, Numbers, Comma (To Separate Phrases and Clauses), Capitalization**

At one time someone in the united states dyed of Cancer every ninety seconds.

■ **Using the Right Word, Wordy Sentence**

Cold water is heavier then hot water and weighs more as well.

■ **Capitalization, Subject-Verb Agreement, Comma (To Separate Adjectives), Colon**

The flat wide rings of saturn is thin less than two miles thick.

WEEK 5: Corrected Sentences

- **Comma (Series and Unnecessary), Using the Right Word**

  The parachute was used in 1783 to save people, ~~whom~~ *who* had to jump from burning buildings, high towers, and other dangerous places.

- **Using the Right Word, Numbers, Spelling**

  Earth moves ~~threw~~ *through* space ~~8~~ *eight* times faster than a speeding ~~bullit~~ *bullet*.

- **Using the Right Word, Numbers, Comma (To Separate Phrases and Clauses), Capitalization**

  At one time, someone in the *U*nited *S*tates ~~dyed~~ *died* of *C*ancer every ~~ninety~~ *90* seconds.

- **Using the Right Word, Wordy Sentence**

  Cold water is heavier ~~then~~ *than* hot water ~~and weighs more as well.~~

- **Capitalization, Subject-Verb Agreement, Comma (To Separate Adjectives), Colon**

  The flat, wide rings of *S*aturn ~~is~~ *are* thin: less than two miles thick.

WEEK 6: Science and Scientists

■ **Comma (Unnecessary and Appositives), Apostrophe, Subject-Verb Agreement**

Thomas Edison one of the world's greatest inventors were deaf from the age of 12, and didnt go to school.

■ **Italics and Underlining, Capitalization, Quotation Marks**

alice of Alice in Wonderland said, if you drink from a bottle marked 'poison,' it is almost certain to disagree with you, sooner or later.

■ **Comma (Numbers), Parentheses, Hyphen (Single-Thought Adjectives), Verb (Tense)**

Light moved at such an out of this world rate 186000 miles per second that it doesn't seem to move at all.

■ **Comma (To Separate Phrases and Clauses), Parentheses**

When crossing tall and short pea plants Gregor Mendel discovered the existence of genetic traits dominant and recessive.

■ **Comma (To Separate Phrases and Clauses), Using the Right Word**

According to modern physics going faster then the speed of light wood move you backward in time.

WEEK 6: Corrected Sentences

■ **Comma (Unnecessary and Appositives), Apostrophe, Subject-Verb Agreement**

Thomas Edison, one of the world's greatest inventors, *was* ~~were~~ deaf from the age of 12, and didn't go to school.

■ **Italics and Underlining, Capitalization, Quotation Marks**

*A*lice of <u>Alice in Wonderland</u> said, "If you drink from a bottle marked 'poison,' it is almost certain to disagree with you, sooner or later."

■ **Comma (Numbers), Parentheses, Hyphen (Single-Thought Adjectives), Verb (Tense)**

Light *moves* ~~moved~~ at such an out-of-this-world rate (186,000 miles per second) that it doesn't seem to move at all.

■ **Comma (To Separate Phrases and Clauses), Parentheses**

When crossing tall and short pea plants, Gregor Mendel discovered the existence of genetic traits (dominant and recessive).

■ **Comma (To Separate Phrases and Clauses), Using the Right Word**

According to modern physics, going faster *than* ~~then~~ the speed of light *would* ~~wood~~ move you backward in time.

WEEK 7: Big and Strange

■ **Adjective (Comparative/Superlative), Subject-Verb Agreement, Plurals**

The most large whale ever reported were 106 foots long.

■ **Comma (To Separate Phrases and Clauses), Apostrophe (Possessives), Numbers**

Although a whales heart can be as big as a car it beats only 9 times a minute.

■ **Using the Right Word, Subject-Verb Agreement, Numbers, Run-On Sentence**

Since nineteen hundred about three hundred fifty thousand blew whales has been killed by whale hunters the whales could face extinction.

■ **Numbers, Subject-Verb Agreement, Hyphen (Single-Thought Adjectives)**

1,400 whales is killed each year by greed driven whale hunters.

■ **Verb (Irregular), Run-On Sentence, Hyphen (Single-Thought Adjectives), Plurals**

In the Galápagos Island's, Darwin watched a blue-footed booby as it swimmed in shallow water the booby is a funny looking fishing bird.

WEEK 7: Corrected Sentences

■ **Adjective (Comparative/Superlative), Subject-Verb Agreement, Plurals**

The ~~most large~~ *largest* whale ever reported ~~were~~ *was* 106 ~~foots~~ *feet* long.

■ **Comma (To Separate Phrases and Clauses), Apostrophe (Possessives), Numbers**

Although a whale*'s* heart can be as big as a car*,* it beats only ~~9~~ *nine* times

a minute.

■ **Using the Right Word, Subject-Verb Agreement, Numbers, Run-On Sentence**

Since ~~nineteen hundred~~ *1900* about ~~three hundred fifty thousand~~ *350,000* ~~blew~~ *blue* whales

~~has~~ *have* been killed by whale hunters*so* the whales could face extinction.

■ **Numbers, Subject-Verb Agreement, Hyphen (Single-Thought Adjectives)**

Fourteen hundred
~~1,400~~ whales ~~is~~ *are* killed each year by greed*-*driven whale hunters.

■ **Verb (Irregular), Run-On Sentence, Hyphen (Single-Thought Adjectives), Plurals**

In the Galápagos ~~Island's~~ *Islands*, Darwin watched a blue-footed booby as it

~~swimmed~~ *swam* in shallow water*. T*he booby is a funny*-*looking fishing bird.

WEEK 8: Land, Water, and Air

■ **Subject-Verb Agreement, Using the Right Word, Comma (Unnecessary), Apostrophe (Possessives)**

Did you no, a yaks milk are pink?

■ **Numbers, Subject-Verb Agreement, Using the Right Word**

Our biology teacher learned us that vampire bats drinks up to 46 pints of blood in 1 year.

■ **Using the Right Word, Apostrophe, Hyphen**

The bee hummingbird lies an egg thats about one third of an inch long.

■ **Comma (To Separate Phrases and Clauses), Misplaced Modifier, Capitalization**

The Pacific leatherback turtle is the largest sea turtle known to Marine biologists weighing up to 1,000 pounds.

■ **Using the Right Word, Double Negative, Apostrophe, Double Subject**

A crocodile it doesnt never chew its food—it swallows it hole.

WEEK 8: Corrected Sentences

■ **Subject-Verb Agreement, Using the Right Word, Comma (Unnecessary), Apostrophe (Possessives)**

Did you ~~no,~~ *know* a yak's milk ~~are~~ *is* pink?

■ **Numbers, Subject-Verb Agreement, Using the Right Word**

Our biology teacher ~~learned~~ *taught* us that vampire bats ~~drinks~~ *drink* up to 46 pints of blood in ~~1~~ *one* year.

■ **Using the Right Word, Apostrophe, Hyphen**

The bee hummingbird ~~lies~~ *lays* an egg that's about one-third of an inch long.

■ **Comma (To Separate Phrases and Clauses), Misplaced Modifier, Capitalization**

Weighing up to 1,000 pounds,
The Pacific leatherback turtle is the largest sea turtle known to *m*arine biologists. ~~weighing up to 1,000 pounds.~~

■ **Using the Right Word, Double Negative, Apostrophe, Double Subject**

A crocodile ~~it~~ doesn't ~~never~~ *(or) ever* chew its food—it swallows it ~~hole~~ *whole*.

WEEK 9: Animals Wild and Tame

- **Comma (To Separate Adjectives and Between Independent Clauses), Verb (Irregular)**

  A beaver's teeth never stop growing but they get weared down when the beaver chews on hard rough bark.

- **Using the Right Word, Quotation Marks, Comma (To Enclose Information)**

  A squirrel seas only in black and white, Ralph Lando PhD reported.

- **End Punctuation, Spelling, Parentheses**

  Would you beleive a snake smells with its tongue and a sense organ on the roof of its mouth Jacobson's organ.

- **Pronoun-Antecedent Agreement, Pronoun (Reflexive)**

  Besides panting, dogs sweat through the pads of its feet to cool their selves off.

- **Using the Right Word, Dash, Subject-Verb Agreement**

  Mail monkeys goes bald as they get older just as some men does.

WEEK 9: Corrected Sentences

■ **Comma (To Separate Adjectives and Between Independent Clauses), Verb (Irregular)**

A beaver's teeth never stop growing‸ but they get ~~weared~~ *worn* down when the

beaver chews on hard‸ rough bark.

■ **Using the Right Word, Quotation Marks, Comma (To Enclose Information)**

‟A squirrel ~~seas~~ *sees* only in black and white‟ Ralph Lando‸ PhD‸ reported.

■ **End Punctuation, Spelling, Parentheses**

Would you ~~beleive~~ *believe* a snake smells with its tongue and a sense organ on

the roof of its mouth‸ (Jacobson's organ)?

■ **Pronoun-Antecedent Agreement, Pronoun (Reflexive)**

Besides panting, dogs sweat through the pads of ~~its~~ *their* feet to cool

~~their selves~~ *themselves* off.

■ **Using the Right Word, Dash, Subject-Verb Agreement**

~~Mail~~ *Male* monkeys ~~goes~~ *go* bald as they get older‸—just as some men ~~does~~ *do*.

WEEK 10: Animals Great and Small

■ **Using the Right Word, Parentheses, End Punctuation, Capitalization, Interjection**

The average hummingbird there are 19 varieties in the United States ways less then a penny, wow.

■ **Using the Right Word, Run-On Sentence, Apostrophe (Possessives), Adjective (Articles)**

A baby kangaroo is only about a inch long at berth it can survive only in it's mothers pouch.

■ **Subject-Verb Agreement, Using the Right Word**

Fore every human being in the world, there is too chickens.

■ **Subject-Verb Agreement, Capitalization, End Punctuation**

White sharks never get sick and is completely immune to Cancer

■ **Comma (To Separate Adjectives and To Separate Phrases and Clauses), Using the Right Word, End Punctuation**

If a goldfish is kept in the dark will it loose it's bright wonderful color.

WEEK 10: Corrected Sentences

■ **Using the Right Word, Parentheses, End Punctuation, Capitalization, Interjection**

The average hummingbird (there are 19 varieties in the United States)
weighs *than* *W* *!*
~~ways~~ less ~~then~~ a penny. ~~wow~~

■ **Using the Right Word, Run-On Sentence, Apostrophe (Possessives), Adjective (Articles)**

an *birth (or) .* *l*
A baby kangaroo is only about ~~a~~ inch long at ~~berth~~; it can survive only in
its *v*
~~it's~~ mothers pouch.

■ **Subject-Verb Agreement, Using the Right Word**

For *are two*
~~Fore~~ every human being in the world, there ~~is~~ ~~too~~ chickens.

■ **Subject-Verb Agreement, Capitalization, End Punctuation**

are *c* *! (or) .*
White sharks never get sick and ~~is~~ completely immune to ~~c~~ancer

■ **Comma (To Separate Adjectives and To Separate Phrases and Clauses), Using the Right Word, End Punctuation**

lose its
If a goldfish is kept in the dark, will it ~~loose~~ ~~it's~~ bright, wonderful color?

WEEK 11: Animals and Insects

■ **Using the Right Word, Subject-Verb Agreement**

Every year millions of trees are planted by squirrels who buries nuts and then forgets ware they put them.

■ **Using the Right Word, Parallelism, Plurals**

Sum kindes of ants rule other ants; they attack them, kidnap them, and then are keeping them as slaves.

■ **Using the Right Word, Adjective (Articles), Pronoun (Reflexive)**

A aunt can lift 50 times its own wait all by himself.

■ **Using the Right Word, Comma (Between Independent Clauses)**

Ants wake up in the mourning and they yawn and stretch before going off too work.

■ **Comma (Unnecessary), Using the Right Word**

A cockroach, can live four several weaks without it's head.

WEEK 11: Corrected Sentences

■ **Using the Right Word, Subject-Verb Agreement**

Every year millions of trees are planted by squirrels ~~who~~ *that* ~~buries~~ *bury* nuts and

then ~~forgets~~ ~~ware~~ *forget where* they put them.

■ **Using the Right Word, Parallelism, Plurals**

Some kinds
~~Sum~~ ~~kindes~~ of ants rule other ants; they attack them, kidnap them, and

~~then~~ ~~are~~ *keep* ~~keeping~~ them as slaves.

■ **Using the Right Word, Adjective (Articles), Pronoun (Reflexive)**

An ant   *weight*   *itself*
~~A~~ ~~aunt~~ can lift 50 times its own ~~wait~~ all by ~~himself~~.

■ **Using the Right Word, Comma (Between Independent Clauses)**

morning
Ants wake up in the ~~mourning~~, and they yawn and stretch before going

to
off ~~too~~ work.

■ **Comma (Unnecessary), Using the Right Word**

for   *weeks*   *its*
A cockroach, can live ~~four~~ several ~~weaks~~ without ~~it's~~ head.

WEEK 12: Amazing Creatures

■ **Capitalization, Quotation Marks**

Mr. Walters told us that "A starfish is the only animal able to turn its stomach inside out."

■ **Using the Right Word, Apostrophe (Possessives)**

The great white sharks teeth are as hard as steal.

■ **Comma (To Separate Phrases and Clauses), Verb (Irregular), Hyphen (Single-Thought Adjectives)**

When their troop carrying steamship sank off the coast of South Africa in 1942 about 700 men were ate by sharks.

■ **Comma (To Separate Phrases and Clauses), Plurals, Numbers, Adjective (Comparative/Superlative)**

Measuring almost five inchs long the Goliath beetle is the most big bug in the world.

■ **Using the Right Word, Parallelism**

Centipedes have alot of legs, two poison fangs, and they have three pears of jaws.

WEEK 12: Corrected Sentences

■ **Capitalization, Quotation Marks**

Mr. Walters told us that "*a* A starfish is the only animal able to turn its

stomach inside out."

■ **Using the Right Word, Apostrophe (Possessives)**

The great white shark's teeth are as hard as ~~steal~~ *steel*.

■ **Comma (To Separate Phrases and Clauses), Verb (Irregular),
Hyphen (Single-Thought Adjectives)**

When their troop-carrying steamship sank off the coast of South Africa in

1942, about 700 men were ~~ate~~ *eaten* by sharks.

■ **Comma (To Separate Phrases and Clauses), Plurals, Numbers,
Adjective (Comparative/Superlative)**

Measuring almost ~~five inchs~~ *5 inches* long, the Goliath beetle is the ~~most big~~ *biggest* bug

in the world.

■ **Using the Right Word, Parallelism**

Centipedes have ~~alot~~ *a lot* of legs, two poison fangs, and ~~they have~~ three ~~pears~~ *pairs*

of jaws.

WEEK 13: Geography Facts

■ **Using the Right Word, Subject-Verb Agreement, Numbers, Capitalization**

date-palm trees, a source of wealth, is past down from 1 generation too the next in iraq.

■ **Misplaced Modifier, Comma (Series)**

Most of the people are farmers who raise wheat barley cotton and rice who live in Iraq.

■ **Capitalization, Apostrophe (Possessives), Pronoun-Antecedent Agreement**

indias real name is bharat, and their capital is new delhi.

■ **Subject-Verb Agreement, Comma (Dialogue and Direct Address), Quotation Marks**

Class people who live in Argentina eats more meat than people anywhere else in the world said Ms. Latitude to the students.

■ **Using the Right Word, Capitalization, Combining Sentences**

hawaii is further South than florida. Florida is farther south then california.

WEEK 13: Corrected Sentences

■ **Using the Right Word, Subject-Verb Agreement, Numbers, Capitalization**

D
date-palm trees, a source of wealth, ~~is past~~ *are passed* down from ~~1~~ *one* generation ~~too~~ *to*

I
the next in Iraq.

■ **Misplaced Modifier, Comma (Series)**

who live in Iraq
Most of the people∧are farmers who raise wheat∧barley∧cotton∧and rice.

~~who live in Iraq.~~

■ **Capitalization, Apostrophe (Possessives), Pronoun-Antecedent Agreement**

I '   *B*   *its*   *N D*
India's real name is Bharat, and ~~their~~ capital is New Delhi.

■ **Subject-Verb Agreement, Comma (Dialogue and Direct Address), Quotation Marks**

"   *eat*
Class∧people who live in Argentina ~~eats~~ more meat than people anywhere

"
else in the world∧said Ms. Latitude to the students.

■ **Using the Right Word, Capitalization, Combining Sentences**

H   *farther s*   *F , which*   *than*
Hawaii is ~~further~~ South than Florida∧Florida is farther south ~~then~~

C
California.

WEEK 14: Where in the World?

- **Using the Right Word, Plurals, Subject-Verb Agreement, Abbreviations**

  There is a dessert in AK that have sand dunes more than 100 foot high.

- **Abbreviations, Capitalization, Adjective (Comparative/Superlative), Double Subject**

  the ice cap of antarctica it is the world's plentifulest supply of fresh H_2O.

- **Capitalization, Subject-Verb Agreement, End Punctuation**

  In the Country of Bangladesh, many people lives to be only about 61

  years old

- **Subject-Verb Agreement, Comma (To Separate Adjectives), Using the Right Word**

  Greenland is covered buy a thick hard layer of ice that never melt.

- **Capitalization, Verb (Tense), Rambling Sentence, Quotation Marks**

  My grandmother in California made jewelry and she tells me, pure Gold,

  like clay, is so soft that it can be molded with your hands and it is

  mixed with harder metals to make jewelry and other items.

WEEK 14: Corrected Sentences

■ **Using the Right Word, Plurals, Subject-Verb Agreement, Abbreviations**

               desert   Alaska   has   *feet*

There is a ~~dessert~~ in ~~AK~~ that ~~have~~ sand dunes more than 100 ~~foot~~ high.

■ **Abbreviations, Capitalization, Adjective (Comparative/Superlative), Double Subject**

  T   *A*   *most plentiful*   *water*

~~t~~he ice cap of ~~a~~ntarctica ~~it~~ is the world's ~~plentifulest~~ supply of fresh ~~H_2O~~.

■ **Capitalization, Subject-Verb Agreement, End Punctuation**

       c   *live*

In the ~~C~~ountry of Bangladesh, many people ~~lives~~ to be only about 61

              ! (or) ⊙

years old ∧

■ **Subject-Verb Agreement, Comma (To Separate Adjectives), Using the Right Word**

                        by   *melts*

Greenland is covered ~~buy~~ a thick∧hard layer of ice that never ~~melt~~.

■ **Capitalization, Verb (Tense), Rambling Sentence, Quotation Marks**

                      makes   *S*   *"P*   *g*

My grandmother in California ~~made~~ jewelry. ~~and~~ ~~s~~he tells me, ~~p~~ure ~~G~~old,

like clay, is so soft that it can be molded with your hands. ~~and~~ ~~i~~t is

                                                "

mixed with harder metals to make jewelry and other items.

WEEK 15: Around the World

■ **Capitalization, Using the Right Word, Hyphen (Single-Thought Adjectives)**

the great wall of china is the only man made structure that can be scene from space with the naked eye.

■ **End Punctuation, Capitalization, Misplaced Modifier**

did you know that people in Ancient China would build their towns from the air to look like animals.

■ **Using the Right Word, Comma Splice, End Punctuation**

The Dead Sea is the saltiest body of water in the world, it's nine times saltier then the ocean

■ **Using the Right Word, Capitalization, Run-On Sentence**

While we were in the grand canyon, I fell off a mule my mother asked, "Are you alright?"

■ **Comma (Numbers and Addresses), Verb (Irregular), Spelling**

In 1868, about 100000 meterites falled on Pultusk Poland in just one night.

WEEK 15: Corrected Sentences

- **Capitalization, Using the Right Word, Hyphen (Single-Thought Adjectives)**

*T**T**he **G**great **W**wall of **C**china is the only man-made structure that can be ~~scene~~ *seen* from space with the naked eye.

- **End Punctuation, Capitalization, Misplaced Modifier**

*D**D**id you know that people in *a*Ancient China would build their towns ~~from the air~~ to look like animals *from the air?*

- **Using the Right Word, Comma Splice, End Punctuation**

The Dead Sea is the saltiest body of water in the world, *(or) .* it's nine times saltier ~~then~~ *than* the ocean *! (or) .*

- **Using the Right Word, Capitalization, Run-On Sentence**

While we were in the *G*grand *C*canyon, I fell off a mule. *M*my mother asked, "Are you ~~alright~~ *all right*?"

- **Comma (Numbers and Addresses), Verb (Irregular), Spelling**

In 1868, about 100,000 ~~meterites~~ *meteorites* ~~falled~~ *fell* on Pultusk, Poland, in just one night.

WEEK 16: Baseball and Football Facts

■ **Double Subject, Misplaced Modifier**

In 1993, a man he was the first person, born without a right hand, named Jim Abbott to pitch a no-hitter in the major leagues.

■ **Subject-Verb Agreement, Capitalization, Adjective (Articles)**

no woman have ever played in an Major-League Baseball game.

■ **Numbers, Using the Right Word, Verb (Irregular), Plurals**

In 1919, 8 player on the Chicago White Sox taked money from gamblers to loose the World Series on purpose.

■ **Capitalization, Comma (Dates), Sentence Fragment**

on April 8 1975, frank robinson the first black major-league baseball manager.

■ **Capitalization, Run-On Sentence, Using the Right Word**

the first Super Bowl was played in 1967 at the los angeles coliseum the Green Bay packers beet the Kansas City chiefs.

WEEK 16: Corrected Sentences

■ **Double Subject, Misplaced Modifier**

Jim Abbott
In 1993, ~~a man he~~ was the first person, born without a right hand,

~~named Jim Abbott~~ to pitch a no-hitter in the major leagues.

■ **Subject-Verb Agreement, Capitalization, Adjective (Articles)**

N   has   a m   l   b
no woman ~~have~~ ever played in ~~an~~ Major-League Baseball game.

■ **Numbers, Using the Right Word, Verb (Irregular), Plurals**

eight players   *took*
In 1919, ~~8 player~~ on the Chicago White Sox ~~taked~~ money from gamblers

lose
to ~~loose~~ the World Series on purpose.

■ **Capitalization, Comma (Dates), Sentence Fragment**

O   F   R   *became*
On April 8, 1975, frank robinson the first black major-league baseball

manager.

■ **Capitalization, Run-On Sentence, Using the Right Word**

T   L   A   C   (or) ⊙T
the first Super Bowl was played in 1967 at the los angeles coliseum the

P   *beat*   C
Green Bay packers ~~beet~~ the Kansas City chiefs.

© Houghton Mifflin Harcourt Publishing Company

WEEK 17: Sports Firsts and Facts

■ **Numbers, Abbreviations, Verb (Tense)**

At one time, about sixty-five % of the members of the National Basketball Association are African American.

■ **Comma (Addresses and Nonrestrictive Phrases and Clauses), Numbers**

The first female jockey was Alicia Meynell who won 2 races in York England in 1804.

■ **Comma (Appositives), Numbers, Using the Right Word, Spelling**

Isaac Murphy a famous African American jocky was the first man too win the Kentucky Derby 3 times.

■ **Numbers, Comma (Dates), Semicolon, Subject-Verb Agreement**

The first Indianapolis 500 was held on May 30 1911 the prize were 25,000 dollars.

■ **Comma (Numbers and Nonrestrictive Phrases and Clauses)**

In 1927, Violet Cordery became the first woman to drive around the world traveling 10266 miles at 24 miles per hour.

WEEK 17: Corrected Sentences

■ **Numbers, Abbreviations, Verb (Tense)**

At one time, about ~~sixty-five~~ *65 percent* % of the members of the National Basketball

Association ~~are~~ *were* African American.

■ **Comma (Addresses and Nonrestrictive Phrases and Clauses), Numbers**

The first female jockey was Alicia Meynell, who won *two* ~~2~~ races in York,

England, in 1804.

■ **Comma (Appositives), Numbers, Using the Right Word, Spelling**

Isaac Murphy, a famous African American *jockey* ~~jocky~~, was the first man *to* ~~too~~ win

the Kentucky Derby *three* ~~3~~ times.

■ **Numbers, Comma (Dates), Semicolon, Subject-Verb Agreement**

The first Indianapolis 500 was held on May 30, 1911; the prize ~~were~~ *was*

$25,000 ~~25,000 dollars~~.

■ **Comma (Numbers and Nonrestrictive Phrases and Clauses)**

In 1927, Violet Cordery became the first woman to drive around the world,

traveling 10,266 miles at 24 miles per hour.

WEEK 18: Sports Personalities

- **Subject-Verb Agreement, Wordy Sentence**

May Sutton Bundy were the first woman to win the Wimbledon Tennis Championship and become the champion.

- **Capitalization, Comma (Appositives)**

anna Taylor a daring middle-aged schoolteacher was the first person ever to ride over niagara falls in a barrel.

- **Quotation Marks, Capitalization, Period**

james J Corbett, ironically known as Gentleman Jim, became the first official Heavyweight Boxing champion.

- **Using the Right Word, Subject-Verb Agreement, Comma Splice**

The earliest ice skates was maid of bone, the first world-famous figure skater was Sonja Henie of Norway.

- **Using the Right Word, Comma (Unnecessary), Italics and Underlining, Pronoun-Antecedent Agreement**

Charles Lindbergh, sored threw the air as a sky diver before, they piloted his famous flight in The Spirit of St. Louis.

WEEK 18: Corrected Sentences

- **Subject-Verb Agreement, Wordy Sentence**

  May Sutton Bundy ~~were~~ *was* the first woman to win the Wimbledon Tennis

  Championship. ~~and become the champion.~~

- **Capitalization, Comma (Appositives)**

  *A*nna Taylor, a daring middle-aged schoolteacher, was the first person ever

  to ride over *N*iagara *F*alls in a barrel.

- **Quotation Marks, Capitalization, Period**

  *J*ames J. Corbett, ironically known as "Gentleman Jim," became the first

  official *h*eavyweight *b*oxing champion.

- **Using the Right Word, Subject-Verb Agreement, Comma Splice**

  The earliest ice skates ~~was maid~~ *were made* of bone. *T*he first world-famous figure

  skater was Sonja Henie of Norway.

- **Using the Right Word, Comma (Unnecessary), Italics and Underlining, Pronoun-Antecedent Agreement**

  Charles Lindbergh, *soared through* ~~sored threw~~ the air as a sky diver before *he* ~~they~~ piloted

  his famous flight in The Spirit of St. Louis.

WEEK 19: The Environment and You

■ **Comma (Nonrestrictive Phrases and Clauses), Combining Sentences, Hyphen (Single-Thought Adjectives)**

Pollution filled smoke rains back to our earth as acid rain. It damages forests and lakes.

■ **Capitalization, Wordy Sentence, Adjective (Articles)**

A pesticide is an chemical used to kill Insects and make them die.

■ **Using the Right Word, Comma (Interruptions), Dash**

The affects of pesticides unfortunately cause many Americans to get sick and some dye.

■ **Comma (To Separate Phrases and Clauses), Using the Right Word, Numbers**

While it takes a soda can about five hundred years to decay a glass bottle may remain unchanged fore a million years.

■ **Subject-Verb Agreement, Pronoun-Antecedent Agreement, Capitalization, Hyphen (Single-Thought Adjectives)**

The Cuyahoga river in cleveland were once so polluted that it had 18 inch grease balls floating in them.

WEEK 19: Corrected Sentences

■ **Comma (Nonrestrictive Phrases and Clauses), Combining Sentences, Hyphen (Single-Thought Adjectives)**

which (or) " . . . rain, damaging . . ."

Pollution-filled smoke rains back to our earth as acid rain, It damages

forests and lakes.

■ **Capitalization, Wordy Sentence, Adjective (Articles)**

a　　　　　　　　　　　　*i*

A pesticide is ~~an~~ chemical used to kill Insects, and make them die.

■ **Using the Right Word, Comma (Interruptions), Dash**

effects

The ~~affects~~ of pesticides, unfortunately, cause many Americans to get sick—

die

and some ~~dye~~.

■ **Comma (To Separate Phrases and Clauses), Using the Right Word, Numbers**

500

While it takes a soda can about ~~five hundred~~ years to decay, a glass

for

bottle may remain unchanged ~~fore~~ a million years.

■ **Subject-Verb Agreement, Pronoun-Antecedent Agreement, Capitalization, Hyphen (Single-Thought Adjectives)**

R　　　　　*C*　　　*was*

The Cuyahoga river in Cleveland ~~were~~ once so polluted that it had

it

18-inch grease balls floating in ~~them~~.

WEEK 20: Pollution Control

■ **Using the Right Word, Capitalization, Verb (Irregular), Combining Sentences**

in 1969, the Cuyahoga river catched fire. It was filled with toxic waist.

■ **Using the Right Word, Subject-Verb Agreement, End Punctuation**

Did you no that over 300,000 knew kinds of chemicals is formulated every

year

■ **Pronoun-Antecedent Agreement, Comma (Unnecessary)**

A person, who smokes a pack of cigarettes a day, puts a half cup of tar

in their lungs each year—and pollutes the air as well.

■ **Apostrophe (Possessives), Comma (Series), Plurals**

Some of Americas toxic waste is dumped illegally into waterways fields

ditchs and sewers.

■ **Comma (Interjections and Numbers), Using the Right Word, Abbreviations**

Seriously there are more then 80000 toxic waist dumps in the U.S.

WEEK 20: Corrected Sentences

■ **Using the Right Word, Capitalization, Verb (Irregular), Combining Sentences**

I ...... *R* .... *caught* .... *because* .... *waste*
~~I~~n 1969, the Cuyahoga ~~r~~iver ~~catched~~ fire. ~~I~~t was filled with toxic ~~waist~~.

■ **Using the Right Word, Subject-Verb Agreement, End Punctuation**

.... *know* .... *new* .... *are*
Did you ~~no~~ that over 300,000 ~~knew~~ kinds of chemicals ~~is~~ formulated every

?
year

■ **Pronoun-Antecedent Agreement, Comma (Unnecessary)**

A person who smokes a pack of cigarettes a day puts a half cup of tar

his or her
in ~~their~~ lungs each year—and pollutes the air as well.

■ **Apostrophe (Possessives), Comma (Series), Plurals**

.... *'*
Some of America~~s~~ toxic waste is dumped illegally into waterways, fields,

ditches
~~ditchs~~, and sewers.

■ **Comma (Interjections and Numbers), Using the Right Word, Abbreviations**

.... *waste* .... *United States.*
Seriously, there are more then 80,000 toxic ~~waist~~ dumps in the ~~U.S.~~

WEEK 21: Air and Water Pollution

■ **Using the Right Word, Comma Splice**

In 1981, a brewery in Washington pored 500,000 gallons of beer into Capitol Lake, about 50,000 fish were found dead one weak later.

■ **Capitalization, Comma (Appositives), Adjective (Comparative/Superlative)**

lake Erie the fourth most large great lake was once declared dead by scientists because it was so polluted.

■ **Abbreviations, Comma (To Separate Phrases and Clauses)**

Without cooling water the temperature inside a nuclear reactor may reach 4,000°.

■ **Subject-Verb Agreement, Abbreviations**

About 407 million gallons of oil is shipped to the U.S. every day.

■ **Using the Right Word, Abbreviations, Verb (Tense)**

Pollution-control laws decrease the amount of led in the air by 55% between 1976 and 1980.

WEEK 21: Corrected Sentences

■ **Using the Right Word, Comma Splice**

In 1981, a brewery in Washington ~~pored~~ *poured* 500,000 gallons of beer into

Capitol Lake ; (or) . A about 50,000 fish were found dead one ~~weak~~ *week* later.

■ **Capitalization, Comma (Appositives), Adjective (Comparative/Superlative)**

*L*ake Erie, the fourth ~~most large~~ *largest* *G*reat *L*ake, was once declared dead by

scientists because it was so polluted.

■ **Abbreviations, Comma (To Separate Phrases and Clauses)**

Without cooling water, the temperature inside a nuclear reactor may

reach 4,000° *degrees* .

■ **Subject-Verb Agreement, Abbreviations**

About 407 million gallons of oil ~~is~~ *are* shipped to the ~~U.S.~~ *United States* every day.

■ **Using the Right Word, Abbreviations, Verb (Tense)**

Pollution-control laws ~~decrease~~ *decreased* the amount of ~~led~~ *lead* in the air by 55~~%~~ *percent*

between 1976 and 1980.

WEEK 22: The American Colonies

■ **Using the Right Word, Numbers, Subject-Verb Agreement**

14 people was executed between the years 1647 and sixteen sixty-two because they were thought to be whiches.

■ **Capitalization, Period, Comma (To Separate Phrases and Clauses)**

in the 1600s a missionary named mr john eliot translated the bible into native american languages.

■ **Using the Right Word, Double Negative, Parallelism, Apostrophe**

In the colonies, most women werent never aloud to go to school, didnt no how to read, and they couldnt vote.

■ **Using the Right Word, Comma (To Separate Phrases and Clauses)**

In 1641 the general court of Massachusetts past a law banning sum religious groups from the colony.

■ **Using the Right Word, Abbreviations, Double Subject**

William Penn he founded Pa. as a place wear Quakers they could practice there religion freely.

WEEK 22: Corrected Sentences

■ **Using the Right Word, Numbers, Subject-Verb Agreement**

Fourteen were   1662
~~14~~ people ~~was~~ executed between the years 1647 and ~~sixteen sixty-two~~

                                    witches
because they were thought to be ~~whiches~~.

■ **Capitalization, Period, Comma (To Separate Phrases and Clauses)**

I   M J   E   B
~~i~~n the 1600s‚ a missionary named m͟r͟. ͟john ͟eliot translated the ͟bible into

N   A
͟native ͟american languages.

■ **Using the Right Word, Double Negative, Parallelism, Apostrophe**

                                           ∨'   ⌐allowed   ∨'know
In the colonies, most women weren͟t ~~never~~ ~~aloud~~ to go to school, didn͟t ~~no~~

how to read, and ~~they~~⌐couldn͟t∨' vote.

■ **Using the Right Word, Comma (To Separate Phrases and Clauses)**

                                                         passed   some
In 1641‚the general court of Massachusetts ~~past~~ a law banning ~~sum~~

religious groups from the colony.

■ **Using the Right Word, Abbreviations, Double Subject**

                       ⌐   Pennsylvania   where
William Penn ~~he~~⌐founded ~~Pa.~~ as a place ~~wear~~ Quakers ~~they~~⌐could practice

their
~~there~~ religion freely.

WEEK 23: The Founding Fathers

- **Adjective (Comparative/Superlative), Sentence Fragment, Comma (Dates)**

  Born on January 17 1706, Benjamin Franklin the most young boy of 17 children and the son of a candlestick maker.

- **Comma (To Separate Phrases and Clauses), Verb (Irregular), Numbers, Spelling**

  Although he had only 2 years of formal edukation Ben Franklin was gived degrees by Harvard, Yale, and Oxford univercities.

- **Capitalization, Using the Right Word, Comma (Series), Pronoun (Reflexive)**

  ben Franklin learned his self french spanish and italian.

- **Comma (Between Independent Clauses), Nonstandard Language, Verb (Irregular), Capitalization**

  the original declaration of independence would of freed all the slaves but Thomas Jefferson taked that part out.

- **Subject-Verb Agreement, Comma (To Separate Phrases and Clauses), Abbreviations**

  When the U.S. were first established as a nation the Congress wanted to make George Washington the king.

WEEK 23: Corrected Sentences

■ **Adjective (Comparative/Superlative), Sentence Fragment, Comma (Dates)**

Born on January 17‸1706, Benjamin Franklin‸the ~~most young~~ *was* *youngest* boy of 17

children and the son of a candlestick maker.

■ **Comma (To Separate Phrases and Clauses), Verb (Irregular), Numbers, Spelling**

Although he had only ~~2~~ *two* years of formal ~~edukation~~‸ *education* Ben Franklin was

~~gived~~ *given* degrees by Harvard, Yale, and Oxford ~~univercities~~ *universities*.

■ **Capitalization, Using the Right Word, Comma (Series), Pronoun (Reflexive)**

*B*en Franklin ~~learned~~ ~~his self~~ *taught himself* *F*rench‸ *S*panish‸and *I*talian.

■ **Comma (Between Independent Clauses), Nonstandard Language, Verb (Irregular), Capitalization**

*T*he original *d*eclaration of *I*ndependence would ~~of~~ *have* freed all the slaves‸but

Thomas Jefferson ~~taked~~ *took* that part out.

■ **Subject-Verb Agreement, Comma (To Separate Phrases and Clauses), Abbreviations**

When the ~~U.S.~~ *United States* ~~were~~ *was* first established as a nation‸the Congress wanted to

make George Washington the king.

WEEK 24: Of Presidents and Daily Life

■ **Using the Right Word, Verb (Irregular)**

In the 1800s, people commonly spit on there floors and taked baths only

once a week.

■ **Apostrophe (Possessives), Colon, Comma (Series)**

George Washingtons famous face appears in the following places on

postage stamps on dollar bills and on quarters.

■ **Adjective (Comparative/Superlative), Wordy Sentence, Dash**

Abraham Lincoln was the most tall president of the United States 6 feet

4 inches and no president has been taller.

■ **Subject-Verb Agreement, Spelling**

In 1860, Abe Lincoln were elected the first Republican president of the

countrey.

■ **Using the Right Word, Comma (Unnecessary)**

Lincoln was sew unpopular in the South that six states left the Union,

before he even had a chance too move into the White House.

WEEK 24: Corrected Sentences

■ **Using the Right Word, Verb (Irregular)**

(or) spat   *their*   *took*
In the 1800s, people commonly spit on ~~there~~ floors and ~~taked~~ baths only

once a week.

■ **Apostrophe (Possessives), Colon, Comma (Series)**

George Washington's famous face appears in the following places on

postage stamps on dollar bills and on quarters.

■ **Adjective (Comparative/Superlative), Wordy Sentence, Dash**

tallest
Abraham Lincoln was the ~~most tall~~ president of the United States 6 feet

4 inches, ~~and no president has been taller.~~

■ **Subject-Verb Agreement, Spelling**

was
In 1860, Abe Lincoln ~~were~~ elected the first Republican president of the

country
~~countrey.~~

■ **Using the Right Word, Comma (Unnecessary)**

so
Lincoln was ~~sew~~ unpopular in the South that six states left the Union

to
before he even had a chance ~~too~~ move into the White House.

WEEK 25: Facts from American History

■ **Using the Right Word, Comma (To Separate Phrases and Clauses)**

After emancipation Lincoln suggested that freed blacks immigrate from America two Africa.

■ **Numbers, Capitalization, Plurals**

there were more than 620 thousand casualtys in the civil war.

■ **Verb (Irregular), Capitalization, Numbers**

George custer becomed a General in the united states army at the age of twenty-three.

■ **Comma (Series and To Separate Phrases and Clauses), Capitalization, Plurals**

in 1900 more than 76 million mans womans and childs lived in the united states.

■ **Period, Apostrophe (Possessives), Spelling**

Susan B Anthony was one of the first leeders in the womens rights movement.

WEEK 25: Corrected Sentences

■ **Using the Right Word, Comma (To Separate Phrases and Clauses)**

After emancipation, Lincoln suggested that freed blacks ~~immigrate~~ *emigrate* from America ~~two~~ *to* Africa.

■ **Numbers, Capitalization, Plurals**

*T*here were more than ~~620 thousand~~ *620,000* ~~casualtys~~ *casualties* in the *C*ivil *W*ar.

■ **Verb (Irregular), Capitalization, Numbers**

George *C*uster ~~becomed~~ *became* a *G*eneral in the *U*nited *S*tates *A*rmy at the age of ~~twenty-three~~ *23*.

■ **Comma (Series and To Separate Phrases and Clauses), Capitalization, Plurals**

*I*n 1900, more than 76 million ~~mans~~ *men*, ~~womans~~ *women*, and ~~childs~~ *children* lived in the *U*nited *S*tates.

■ **Period, Apostrophe (Possessives), Spelling**

Susan B. Anthony was one of the first ~~leeders~~ *leaders* in the women's rights movement.

WEEK 26: Modern American History

- **Comma (Nonrestrictive Phrases and Clauses), Pronoun (Reflexive), Capitalization**

  Though it's not the type of honor most people would seek for theirself, woodrow wilson who was the president during world war I is the only president buried in washington, D.C.

- **Using the Right Word, Comma (Dates and Addresses), Adjective (Articles)**

  On August 6 1945, the United States dropped a atomic bomb on Hiroshima Japan, and then dropped another on Nagasaki several days latter.

- **Comma (To Enclose Information), Numbers, Spelling**

  In nineteen sixty-four, Martin Luther King Jr. won the Nobel Peace Prise for leading nonviolent, civil-rights protests.

- **Using the Right Word, Capitalization**

  while in High School, Martin Luther King, Jr., did so good that he skipped too grades.

- **Using the Right Word, Comma (To Separate Phrases and Clauses), Capitalization**

  beside finishing college at the young age of 19 Martin Luther King, Jr., became a Minister that same year.

WEEK 26: Corrected Sentences

■ **Comma (Nonrestrictive Phrases and Clauses), Pronoun (Reflexive), Capitalization**

Though it's not the type of honor most people would seek for ~~theirself~~ *themselves*,

Woodrow **W**ilson, who was the president during **W**orld **W**ar I, is the only

president buried in **W**ashington, D.C.

■ **Using the Right Word, Comma (Dates and Addresses), Adjective (Articles)**

On August 6, 1945, the United States dropped ~~a~~ *an* atomic bomb on Hiroshima,

Japan, and then dropped another on Nagasaki several days ~~latter~~ *later*.

■ **Comma (To Enclose Information), Numbers, Spelling**

In ~~nineteen sixty-four~~ *1964*, Martin Luther King, Jr., won the Nobel Peace ~~Prise~~ *Prize*

for leading nonviolent, civil-rights protests.

■ **Using the Right Word, Capitalization**

While in **h**igh **s**chool, Martin Luther King, Jr., did so ~~good~~ *well* that he

skipped ~~too~~ *two* grades.

■ **Using the Right Word, Comma (To Separate Phrases and Clauses), Capitalization**

~~beside~~ *Besides* finishing college at the young age of 19, Martin Luther King, Jr.,

became a **m**inister that same year.

WEEK 27: Proverbs

■ **Using the Right Word, Quotation Marks, Comma (Dialogue and Appositives)**

Thomas Paine a friend of Ben Franklin's wrote It is necessary too the happiness of man that he bee mentally faithful two himself.

■ **Quotation Marks, Subject-Verb Agreement, Capitalization, Comma (Dialogue)**

Abraham Lincoln once said let us have faith that right make might.

■ **Using the Right Word, Spelling**

Beleive nothing of what you here, and only half of what you sea.

■ **Adjective (Comparative/Superlative), Using the Right Word**

It is more good to be born lucky then rich.

■ **Adjective (Articles), Subject-Verb Agreement, Comma (Direct Address)**

An bully are always a coward Henry.

WEEK 27: Corrected Sentences

■ **Using the Right Word, Quotation Marks, Comma (Dialogue and Appositives)**

Thomas Paine_, a friend of Ben Franklin's_, wrote_, "It is necessary *to* ~~too~~ the

happiness of man that he *be* ~~bee~~ mentally faithful *to* ~~two~~ himself."

■ **Quotation Marks, Subject-Verb Agreement, Capitalization, Comma (Dialogue)**

Abraham Lincoln once said_, "*L*et us have faith that right *makes* ~~make~~ might."

■ **Using the Right Word, Spelling**

Believe
~~Beleive~~ nothing of what you *hear* ~~here~~, and only half of what you *see* ~~sea~~.

■ **Adjective (Comparative/Superlative), Using the Right Word**

It is *better* ~~more good~~ to be born lucky *than* ~~then~~ rich.

■ **Adjective (Articles), Subject-Verb Agreement, Comma (Direct Address)**

A
~~An~~ bully *is* ~~are~~ always a coward_, Henry.

WEEK 28: More Proverbs

■ **Using the Right Word, Double Negative, Verb (Tense)**

The coarse of true love never did hardly ran smooth.

—Shakespeare

■ **Comma (Unnecessary), Adjective (Articles), Capitalization**

an teacher, is better than two books.

■ **Comma (Series), Using the Right Word, Verb (Tense)**

Early too bed and early too rise made a man healthy wealthy and wise.

—Ben Franklin

■ **Using the Right Word, Apostrophe, Quotation Marks**

You might accept a librarian to say, Dont judge a book by it's cover.

■ **Using the Right Word, Double Subject, Apostrophe**

Those whom live in glass houses they shouldnt throw stones.

WEEK 28: Corrected Sentences

■ **Using the Right Word, Double Negative, Verb (Tense)**

The ~~coarse~~ *course* of true love never did ~~hardly~~ ~~ran~~ *run* smooth.

—Shakespeare

■ **Comma (Unnecessary), Adjective (Articles), Capitalization**

~~an~~ *A* teacher is better than two books.

■ **Comma (Series), Using the Right Word, Verb (Tense)**

Early ~~too~~ *to* bed and early ~~too~~ *to* rise ~~made~~ *makes* a man healthy, wealthy, and wise.

—Ben Franklin

■ **Using the Right Word, Apostrophe, Quotation Marks**

You might ~~accept~~ *expect* a librarian to say, "Don't judge a book by ~~it's~~ *its* cover."

■ **Using the Right Word, Double Subject, Apostrophe**

Those ~~whom~~ *who* live in glass houses ~~they~~ shouldn't throw stones.

WEEK 29: A Taste of World History

■ **Using the Right Word, Verb (Irregular), Comma Splice**

In ancient China, mouse meet was eated by rich people, they liked it.

■ **Capitalization, Apostrophe, Spelling, Comma (Appositives)**

King alexander III of macedon alexander the great ordered his soljers to shave their heads and faces so that enemies couldnt grab them by the hair.

■ **Capitalization, Comma (Appositives)**

attila the Hun Leader of the Hunnic Empire attacked the roman empire around the year 450.

■ **Capitalization, Subject-Verb Agreement, Semicolon, Plurals**

.attila the hun are believed to have been rather short he stood barely three and one-half foot tall.

■ **Italics and Underlining, Adjective (Articles), Quotation Marks, Run-On Sentence, Using the Right Word**

Muhammad was a Arab preacher whom started the religion called Islam the word Islam means submission.

WEEK 29: Corrected Sentences

- **Using the Right Word, Verb (Irregular), Comma Splice**

In ancient China, mouse ~~meet~~ *meat* was ~~eated~~ *eaten* by rich people; (or .) they liked it.

- **Capitalization, Apostrophe, Spelling, Comma (Appositives)**

King *A*lexander III of *M*acedon, *A*lexander the *G*reat, ordered his ~~soljers~~ *soldiers* to shave their heads and faces so that enemies couldn't grab them by the hair.

- **Capitalization, Comma (Appositives)**

*A*ttila the Hun, *L*eader of the Hunnic Empire, attacked the *R*oman *E*mpire around the year 450.

- **Capitalization, Subject-Verb Agreement, Semicolon, Plurals**

*A*ttila the *H*un ~~are~~ *is* believed to have been rather short; he stood barely three and one-half ~~foot~~ *feet* tall.

- **Italics and Underlining, Adjective (Articles), Quotation Marks, Run-On Sentence, Using the Right Word**

Muhammad was ~~a~~ *an* Arab preacher ~~whom~~ *who* started the religion called Islam. *T*he word Islam means "submission."

WEEK 30: World-History Dates

- **Hyphen, Using the Right Word, Run-On Sentence**

  Buy around 750, one third of the people in the world had excepted the religion of Islam they were called Muslims.

- **Comma (Interjections and To Separate Phrases and Clauses), Numbers, Verb (Irregular)**

  Well in 1032 Benedict IX becomed pope when he was only eleven years old!

- **Using the Right Word, Comma (Nonrestrictive Phrases and Clauses), Dash**

  The Leaning Tower of Pisa who is maid of marble took 200 years to build from 1173 to 1372.

- **Capitalization, Pronoun (Reflexive), Semicolon, End Punctuation**

  in 1279, kublai khan conquered china he made him the emperor?

- **Using the Right Word, Comma (To Separate Phrases and Clauses), Verb (Irregular)**

  In the late 1200s Marco Polo taked a trip to China who lasted 24 years.

WEEK 30: Corrected Sentences

■ **Hyphen, Using the Right Word, Run-On Sentence**

~~Buy~~ *By* around 750, one-third of the people in the world had ~~excepted~~ *accepted* the

religion of Islam. *T*hey were called Muslims.

■ **Comma (Interjections and To Separate Phrases and Clauses), Numbers, Verb (Irregular)**

Well, in 1032, Benedict IX ~~becomed~~ *became* pope when he was only ~~eleven~~ *11* years

old!

■ **Using the Right Word, Comma (Nonrestrictive Phrases and Clauses), Dash**

The Leaning Tower of Pisa, ~~who~~ *which* is ~~maid~~ *made* of marble, took 200 years to build —

from 1173 to 1372.

■ **Capitalization, Pronoun (Reflexive), Semicolon, End Punctuation**

*I*n 1279, *K*ublai *k*han conquered *C*hina; he made ~~him~~ *himself* the emperor.

■ **Using the Right Word, Comma (To Separate Phrases and Clauses), Verb (Irregular)**

In the late 1200s, Marco Polo ~~taked~~ *took* a trip to China ~~who~~ *that* lasted 24 years.

WEEK 31: Another Look at World History

■ **Using the Right Word, Numbers, Colon, Spelling**

Glasses made to correct week eyesite were invented a long time ago in twelve ninety.

■ **Using the Right Word, Plurals, Comma (To Separate Phrases and Clauses)**

In medieval Japan fashionable womans died there tooths black.

■ **Capitalization, Subject-Verb Agreement**

In the middle ages, animals was tried as witches and publicly executed.

■ **Using the Right Word, Comma (Dialogue), Period, Capitalization, Quotation Marks**

richard III killed his too nephews in 1483 in order to bee king said mr bartz.

■ **Capitalization, Interjection**

Beware The bubonic plague (known as the *Black Death* in europe between 1347 and 1350) could be used in Germ Warfare today.

WEEK 31: Corrected Sentences

■ **Using the Right Word, Numbers, Colon, Spelling**

Glasses made to correct ~~week eyesite~~ *weak eyesight* were invented a long time ago͵ in ⋀:

~~twelve ninety~~ *1290*.

■ **Using the Right Word, Plurals, Comma (To Separate Phrases and Clauses)**

In medieval Japan͵⋀ fashionable ~~womans died there tooths~~ *women dyed their teeth* black.

■ **Capitalization, Subject-Verb Agreement**

In the *M* middle *A* ages, animals ~~was~~ *were* tried as witches and publicly executed.

■ **Using the Right Word, Comma (Dialogue), Period, Capitalization, Quotation Marks**

"*R* ̷richard III killed his ~~too~~ *two* nephews in 1483 in order to ~~bee~~ *be* king͵⋀ said

M B ̷mr. ̷bartz.

■ **Capitalization, Interjection**

Beware͵! The bubonic plague (known as the *Black Death* in *E* ̷europe between

1347 and 1350) could be used in *g* ̷Germ *w* ̷Warfare today.

WEEK 32: The Sixteenth Century

- **Capitalization, Verb (Tense), Comma (To Separate Phrases and Clauses), Using the Right Word**

  in the sixteenth Century the Average Person lives too bee 35 years old.

- **Comma (Addresses), Using the Right Word, Subject-Verb Agreement**

  In 1518, at a banquet in Venice Italy forks was used fore the first time.

- **Verb (Tense), Comma (Nonrestrictive Phrases and Clauses)**

  When Henry VIII became king in 1509, he marries Catherine of Aragon

  who was the wife of the last king of England.

- **Numbers, Comma Splice, Spelling**

  Henry VIII had 6 wives, one outlived him, the rest he either divorced or

  exacuted.

- **Verb (Irregular), Apostrophe (Possessives), Pronoun-Antecedent Agreement, Comma (Appositives)**

  Anne Boleyn Henry VIIIs second wife had a sixth finger on one hand and

  continuously weared a glove to hide them.

WEEK 32: Corrected Sentences

- **Capitalization, Verb (Tense), Comma (To Separate Phrases and Clauses), Using the Right Word**

  ~~I~~n the sixteenth ~~C~~entury, the ~~A~~verage ~~P~~erson ~~lives too bee~~ *lived to be* 35 years old.

- **Comma (Addresses), Using the Right Word, Subject-Verb Agreement**

  In 1518, at a banquet in Venice, Italy, forks ~~was~~ *were* used ~~fore~~ *for* the first time.

- **Verb (Tense), Comma (Nonrestrictive Phrases and Clauses)**

  When Henry VIII became king in 1509, he ~~marries~~ *married* Catherine of Aragon, who ~~was~~ *had been* the wife of the last king of England.

- **Numbers, Comma Splice, Spelling**

  Henry VIII had ~~6~~ *six* wives; (or) . one outlived him, *and* the rest he either divorced or *executed* ~~exacuted~~.

- **Verb (Irregular), Apostrophe (Possessives), Pronoun-Antecedent Agreement, Comma (Appositives)**

  Anne Boleyn, Henry VIII's second wife, had a sixth finger on one hand and continuously ~~weared~~ *wore* a glove to hide ~~them~~ *it*.

WEEK 33: More World History Facts

■ **Using the Right Word, Comma (Numbers and Between Independent Clauses), Rambling Sentence**

Queen Elizabeth I always wore a wig and she owned 3000 dresses and she had red hare and she had pale eyes like her father.

■ **Using the Right Word, Comma (Nonrestrictive Phrases and Clauses), Spelling**

Elizabeth I of England which became queen in 1558 was the dauter of Henry VIII and Anne Boleyn.

■ **Using the Right Word, Capitalization, Subject-Verb Agreement**

during the 1600s in japan, the punishment fore trying to immigrate from the country were death.

■ **Using the Right Word, Numbers, Nonstandard Language, Spelling**

Mozart must of recieved many complements fore writing his first symphony at the age of 9.

■ **Numbers, Run-On Sentence, Hyphen (Single-Thought Adjectives)**

10 million people died during a deadly year long flu epidemic it struck the United States and Europe in 1918.

WEEK 33: Corrected Sentences

■ **Using the Right Word, Comma (Numbers and Between Independent Clauses), Rambling Sentence**

Queen Elizabeth I always wore a wig‚and she owned 3‚000 dresses. ~~and~~

S
~~s~~he had red ~~hare~~ *hair* and ~~she had~~ pale eyes like her father.

■ **Using the Right Word, Comma (Nonrestrictive Phrases and Clauses), Spelling**

who
Elizabeth I of England‚~~which~~ became queen in 1558‚was the ~~dauter~~ *daughter* of

Henry VIII and Anne Boleyn.

■ **Using the Right Word, Capitalization, Subject-Verb Agreement**

D   J   *for*   *emigrate*
~~d~~uring the 1600s in ~~j~~apan, the punishment ~~fore~~ trying to ~~immigrate~~ from

was
the country ~~were~~ death.

■ **Using the Right Word, Numbers, Nonstandard Language, Spelling**

have received   *compliments for*
Mozart must ~~of recieved~~ many ~~complements fore~~ writing his first

nine
symphony at the age of ~~9.~~

■ **Numbers, Run-On Sentence, Hyphen (Single-Thought Adjectives)**

Ten   *(or)* . I
~~10~~ million people died during a deadly year‑long flu epidemic‚it struck

the United States and Europe in 1918.

WEEK 34: Potpourri

- **Capitalization, Verb (Irregular), Using the Right Word, Abbreviations**

  in so. amer., termites are roasted and eated buy the handful like popcorn.

- **Capitalization, Verb (Tense), Apostrophe (Possessives)**

  The Ancient egyptians pillows are made of stone.

- **Quotation Marks, Subject-Verb Agreement, Spelling, Using the Right Word**

  Eskimos has more then 20 different words in their languige that

  mean snow.

- **Italics and Underlining, Adjective (Comparative/Superlative), Colon or Dash, Capitalization**

  The most old letter in the Alphabet is the fifteenth letter o.

- **Using the Right Word, Comma (Unnecessary), Plurals, Wordy Sentence**

  The stationery layer of ice that never moves, that covers Antarctica at the

  South Pole, is more than 6,500 foots thick at its thickest.

WEEK 34: Corrected Sentences

■ **Capitalization, Verb (Irregular), Using the Right Word, Abbreviations**

I | *South America*   *eaten* *by*
~~In~~ ~~so. amer.~~, termites are roasted and ~~eated~~ ~~buy~~ the handful like popcorn.

■ **Capitalization, Verb (Tense), Apostrophe (Possessives)**

   a   *E*   ’   *were*
The ~~A~~ncient ~~e~~gyptians pillows ~~are~~ made of stone.

■ **Quotation Marks, Subject-Verb Agreement, Spelling, Using the Right Word**

       have   *than*   *language*
Eskimos ~~has~~ more ~~then~~ 20 different words in their ~~languige~~ that

mean "snow."

■ **Italics and Underlining, Adjective (Comparative/Superlative), Colon or Dash, Capitalization**

     oldest   *a*   *(or)* —
The ~~most old~~ letter in the ~~A~~lphabet is the fifteenth letter: o.

■ **Using the Right Word, Comma (Unnecessary), Plurals, Wordy Sentence**

   stationary
The ~~stationery~~ layer of ice ~~that never moves~~, that covers Antarctica ~~at the~~

                                    feet
~~South Pole~~, is more than 6,500 ~~foots~~ thick ~~at its thickest~~.

© Houghton Mifflin Harcourt Publishing Company

WEEK 35: Who's Counting?

■ **Comma (Dates), Capitalization, Run-On Sentence**

on september 16 1921 a little boy was born in london he had 14 fingers
and 15 toes.

■ **Comma (Numbers), Verb (Irregular), Pronoun-Antecedent Agreement, Capitalization**

a famous bullfighter named lagartigo slayed 4867 bulls during their
career.

■ **Using the Right Word, Adjective (Comparative/Superlative), Dash**

English has the larger amount of active words about 500,000 of all the
known languages.

■ **Comma (Interjections), Apostrophe (Possessives), End Punctuation, Capitalization**

Hey did you know that tom Cruises full name is Thomas cruise
mapother IV.

■ **Colon, Capitalization, Spelling**

a rainbow is made up of seven collors; Red, Orange, Yellow, Green, Blue,
Indigo, and Violet.

WEEK 35: Corrected Sentences

- **Comma (Dates), Capitalization, Run-On Sentence**

  On September 16, 1921, a little boy was born in London; he had 14 fingers and 15 toes.

- **Comma (Numbers), Verb (Irregular), Pronoun-Antecedent Agreement, Capitalization**

  A famous bullfighter named Lagartigo slew 4,867 bulls during his career.

- **Using the Right Word, Adjective (Comparative/Superlative), Dash**

  English has the largest number of active words—about 500,000—of all the known languages.

- **Comma (Interjections), Apostrophe (Possessives), End Punctuation, Capitalization**

  Hey, did you know that Tom Cruise's full name is Thomas Cruise Mapother IV?

- **Colon, Capitalization, Spelling**

  A rainbow is made up of seven colors: Red, Orange, Yellow, Green, Blue, Indigo, and Violet.

improve punctuate

MUG Shot Paragraphs

The MUG Shot paragraphs are a quick and efficient way to review **m**echanics, **u**sage, and **g**rammar errors each week. These paragraphs can also serve as excellent proofreading exercises. Each paragraph can be corrected and discussed in 8 to 10 minutes.

SPELL edit
capitalize

Implementation and Evaluation

For each set of MUG Shot sentences, there is a corresponding MUG Shot paragraph. The paragraph reviews many of the editing skills covered during the week.

Implementation

A MUG Shot paragraph can be implemented at the end of the week as a review or an evaluation activity. Simply distribute copies of the week's paragraph, and have students make their corrections on the sheet. Students may use the "Editing and Proofreading Marks" in *Write Source* or on page iv in this book as a guide in correcting the MUG Shot paragraph. We suggest that students then discuss their changes (in pairs or in small groups). Afterward, go over the paragraph as a class to make sure that everyone understands the reasons for the changes. (You may want to refer to the corresponding MUG Shot sentences during your discussion.)

An Alternative Approach: Distribute copies of the MUG Shot paragraph along with the edited version. (They appear on the same page in your booklet.) Have students fold the edited version under, and then make their changes. Once they are finished, they can unfold the paper and check their own work.

Evaluation

If you use the paragraphs as an evaluation activity, we recommend that you give students a basic performance score for their work. This score should reflect the number of changes the student has marked correctly (before or after any discussion). The weekly score might also reflect the student's work on corresponding MUG Shot sentences.

WEEK 1: Science Class

■ Subject-Verb Agreement, Apostrophe (Possessives), Using the Right Word, Quotation Marks, Comma (Dialogue and To Separate Phrases and Clauses)

In my third-grade science class, I gave a report on birds circulatory systems. I said A birds heart has four chambers—just like a mammals—and it beat rapidly. Also, birds is warm-blooded. After my report my dad brought in our blue parakeet. Everybody tried to count it's heartbeats. Even using a stethoscope no one could count that fast. Maybe that's why birds are so hyper!

Corrected Paragraph

In my third-grade science class, I gave a report on birds'" circulatory systems. I said "A birds' heart has four chambers—just like a mammals'—and it ~~beat~~ *beats* rapidly. Also, birds ~~is~~ *are* warm-blooded." After my report, my dad brought in our blue parakeet. Everybody tried to count *its* ~~it's~~ heartbeats. Even using a stethoscope, no one could count that fast. Maybe that's why birds are so hyper!

WEEK 2: Water World

■ **Apostrophe (Possessives), Comma (Interjections and Interruptions), Numbers, Capitalization, Abbreviations**

Today I learned that more than 70% of the earth is covered by Oceans, which contain 97% of all the water on earth. Then I found out that the Human Body is 65 percent H_2O. That's when I discovered that ocean water is almost 3 percent salt. Aha I remembered tears and perspiration are salty, too. Now I wonder how salty my bodys water is compared to water in the pacific ocean. Gee wouldn't it be strange if in fact the water in our bodies is saltier than the water in the Oceans?

Corrected Paragraph

Today I learned that more than 70% *percent* of the earth is covered by
o
Øceans, which contain 97% *percent* of all the water on earth. Then I found out
h *b* *water*
that the Human Body is 65 percent H_2O. That's when I discovered
three
that ocean water is almost 3 percent salt. Aha, I remembered tears and
perspiration are salty, too. Now I wonder how salty my body's water is
P *O*
compared to water in the pacific ocean. Gee, wouldn't it be strange if, in
o
fact, the water in our bodies is saltier than the water in the Øceans?

WEEK 3: Calling All . . .

■ **Comma (Series), Using the Right Word, Apostrophe (Possessives), Adverb (Comparative/Superlative), Parentheses**

Scientists are working more hard than ever on voice-activated devices things that respond to a spoken command. Very soon, you're homes computer could be programmed too open a garage door or turn on lights appliances televisions and stereos—every time you tell it to. Since voiceprints are as unique as fingerprints, the computer wood respond to your voice (or the owners) but no one elses. Today their are voice-activated devices for your car, such as door locks keyless ignitions and global location systems.

Corrected Paragraph

Scientists are working ~~more hard~~ *harder* than ever on voice-activated devices (things that respond to a spoken command) Very soon, ~~you're~~ *your* homes' computer could be programmed ~~too~~ *to* open a garage door or turn on lights, appliances, televisions, and stereos—every time you tell it to. Since voiceprints are as unique as fingerprints, the computer ~~wood~~ *would* respond to your voice (or the owners') but no one else's. Today ~~their~~ *there* are voice-activated devices for your car, such as door locks, keyless ignitions, and global location systems.

WEEK 4: Shake a Leg!

■ **Subject-Verb Agreement, Pronoun-Antecedent Agreement, Parallelism, Rambling Sentence, Comma (To Separate Phrases and Clauses)**

The family of plants known as legumes are very important to our ecology. Legumes have nodules on their roots containing bacteria. These bacteria takes nitrogen from the air and changes it into forms that can be used by plants and farmers often use legumes as cover crops to prevent soil erosion and for improving poor soil. Once the plants are grown they provides food for animals and humans. Perhaps you know some legumes by its more common names: peas, beans, peanuts, and clover. By any name legumes are important to us all.

Corrected Paragraph

The family of plants known as legumes ~~are~~ *is* very important to our ecology. Legumes have nodules on their roots containing bacteria. These bacteria ~~takes~~ *take* nitrogen from the air and ~~changes~~ *change* it into forms that can be used by plants. ~~and~~ *F*armers often use legumes as cover crops to prevent soil erosion and ~~for improving~~ *to improve* poor soil. Once the plants are grown, they ~~provides~~ *provide* food for animals and humans. Perhaps you know some legumes by ~~its~~ *their* more common names: peas, beans, peanuts, and clover. By any name, legumes are important to us all.

WEEK 5: Slow Falling

■ **Comma (Series, To Separate Phrases and Clauses, and To Separate Adjectives), Colon, Using the Right Word, Spelling**

Though people experamented with parachutes hundreds of years ago the first known parachute jump was made by a Frenchman in 1783. Since the development of air travel parachutes have been used for other reasons escaping from damaged aircraft dropping troops and supplies into war zones and delivering emergency food and medicine too people who are in need. Today, some thrill seekers can wear parachutes just for fun—in the daring high-flying sport of skydiving.

Corrected Paragraph

Though people ~~experamented~~ *experimented* with parachutes hundreds of years ago, the first known parachute jump was made by a Frenchman in 1783. Since the development of air travel, parachutes have been used for other reasons: escaping from damaged aircraft, dropping troops and supplies into war zones, and delivering emergency food and medicine ~~too~~ *to* people who are in need. Today, some thrill seekers ~~can~~ *may* wear parachutes just for fun—in the daring, high-flying sport of skydiving.

WEEK 6: What Time Is It?

■ **Comma (Unnecessary), Subject-Verb Agreement, Using the Right Word, Italics and Underlining, Hyphen (Single-Thought Adjectives)**

The Time Machine by H. G. Wells is a book about a inventor, whom make a vehicle for traveling in time. If time travel machines was real, people might try too change history. But if even one passed event were changed, would the present be the same? Think about the chain reaction affect one changed event would have on so many people—not just the people present for the event, but the people in the generations who followed, to.

Corrected Paragraph

The Time Machine by H. G. Wells is a book about a̶ **an** inventor,/ w̶h̶o̶m̶ **who**
m̶a̶k̶e̶ **makes** a vehicle for traveling in time. If time‿travel machines w̶a̶s̶ **were** real,
people might try t̶o̶o̶ **to** change history. But if even one p̶a̶s̶s̶e̶d̶ **past** event were
changed, would the present be the same? Think about the chain‿reaction
a̶f̶f̶e̶c̶t̶ **effect** one changed event would have on so many people—not just the
people present for the event, but the people in the generations w̶h̶o̶ **that**
followed, t̶o̶ **too**.

WEEK 7: Save the Whales!

■ **Comma (Appositives and To Separate Phrases and Clauses), Run-On Sentence, Numbers, Apostrophe (Possessives)**

During the last one hundred years about 350,000 blue whales the largest animals that have ever lived have been killed by whale hunters. This slaughters threat has put the whales existence in question. In 1946 the International Whaling Commission was formed to protect whales from overhunting most biologists believe the blue whales have been saved from extinction, but people must continue to protect them.

Corrected Paragraph

During the last ~~one hundred~~ 100 years, about 350,000 blue whales, the largest animals that have ever lived, have been killed by whale hunters. This slaughter's threat has put the whales' existence in question. In 1946, the International Whaling Commission was formed to protect whales from overhunting. Most biologists believe the blue whales have been saved from extinction, but people must continue to protect them.

WEEK 8: Turtle Races

■ **Apostrophe, Using the Right Word, Double Subject, Comma (Unnecessary), Hyphen (Single-Thought Adjective), Misplaced Modifier**

Sea turtles dont have an easy start in life, of which there are seven species. The female sea turtles travel great distances to lie their eggs on the shores, wear they were born. Once the eggs are laid, various animals and birds they try to eat them. As soon as the turtles hatch, theyve got a long distance race to the ocean. Along the way, and even after reaching the water, predators threaten their survival. Fortunately, many sea turtles survive even against these not so great odds.

Corrected Paragraph

of which there are seven species,

Sea turtles don't have an easy start in life, of which there are seven species. The female sea turtles travel great distances to lie *lay* their eggs on the shores, wear *where* they were born. Once the eggs are laid, various animals and birds they try to eat them. As soon as the turtles hatch, they've got a long distance race to the ocean. Along the way, and even after reaching the water, predators threaten their survival. Fortunately, many sea turtles survive even against these not so great odds.

WEEK 9: Seeing Things

■ Subject-Verb Agreement, Pronoun-Antecedent Agreement, Parentheses, Comma (Between Independent Clauses), Spelling

At the Museum of Science and Industry in Chicago, people can looks through amazing lenses that show how various animals sees. Some animals, like squirrels, sees only in black and white. Bees can see ultraviolet light, which is invisable to people but it cannot see red. Crocodiles see colors as different shades of gray. Scientists can determine whether or not an animal sees color by finding cones color vision receptors inside the retina of their eye.

Corrected Paragraph

At the Museum of Science and Industry in Chicago, people can
look
~~looks~~ through amazing lenses that show how various animals ~~sees~~. *see*
see
Some animals, like squirrels, ~~sees~~ only in black and white. Bees can
invisible *they*
see ultraviolet light, which is ~~invisable~~ to people‚ but ~~it~~ cannot see red.
Crocodiles see colors as different shades of gray. Scientists can determine
whether or not an animal sees color by finding cones (color vision
its
receptors) inside the retina of ~~their~~ eye.

WEEK 10: Three Blind Creatures

■ **Comma (To Separate Phrases and Clauses), Using the Right Word, End Punctuation, Capitalization, Run-On Sentence**

Cavefish live in the cool underground waters of echo river inside mammoth cave, kentucky. Not only do these fish lack eyes but there bodies also lack pigmentation. These strange little fish are only three inches long they are pink because their blood shows threw they're flesh. Why don't they have eyes. Living in total darkness the cavefish have no need to see. Other blind creatures living in mammoth cave include Beetles and Crayfish.

Corrected Paragraph

Cavefish live in the cool underground waters of ~~e~~cho ~~r~~iver inside
E R
~~m~~ammoth ~~c~~ave, ~~k~~entucky. Not only do these fish lack eyes , but ~~there~~ *their*
M C K
bodies also lack pigmentation. These strange little fish are only three
inches long. ~~t~~hey are pink because their blood shows ~~threw~~ ~~they're~~ *through their* flesh.
T
Why don't they have eyes ? Living in total darkness , the cavefish have no
need to see. Other blind creatures living in ~~m~~ammoth ~~c~~ave include ~~B~~eetles
M C b
and ~~C~~rayfish.
c

WEEK 11: Hide 'N' Seek

■ **Comma (Between Independent Clauses), Adjective (Articles), Plurals, Pronoun (Reflexive), Parallelism, Using the Right Word**

Squirrels devote lots of time to food—searching for it, burying it, then they search for it again. The seed and nuts they enjoy are scarce in winter but abundant in autumn so they store large food supplys in the ground. Every year milliones of trees are planted by squirrels who bury seeds and nuts and then were forgetting where they put them. But if they have a good memory and an sharp sense of smell, they can retrieve the hidden food for their selfs during a winter.

Corrected Paragraph

Squirrels devote lots of time to food—searching for it, burying it, then ~~they search~~ *searching* for it again. The ~~seed~~ *seeds* and nuts they enjoy are scarce in winter but abundant in autumn, so they store large food ~~supplys~~ *supplies* in the ground. Every year ~~milliones~~ *millions* of trees are planted by squirrels ~~who~~ *that* bury seeds and nuts and then ~~were forgetting~~ *forget* where they put them. But if they have a good memory and ~~an~~ *a* sharp sense of smell, they can retrieve the hidden food for ~~their selfs~~ *themselves* during ~~a~~ *the* winter.

WEEK 12: Shark Attack!

■ **Verb (Irregular), Comma (To Separate Phrases and Clauses), Capitalization, Hyphen (Single-Thought Adjectives), Plurals**

Sharks aren't the best loved animals in the world. When the *nova scotia* sinked off the coast of africa in 1942 about 700 men were killed by sharks. This kind of publicity gived sharks an even worse reputation. People have had a hard time forgiving and forgetting, even though fewer than 100 shark attacks are reported each year, and most attacks do not result in life threatening injurys or death.

Corrected Paragraph

Sharks aren't the best ̄loved animals in the world. When the *Nova Scotia* ~~sinked~~ sank off the coast of ^Africa in 1942, about 700 men were killed by sharks. This kind of publicity ~~gived~~ gave sharks an even worse reputation. People have had a hard time forgiving and forgetting, even though fewer than 100 shark attacks are reported each year, and most attacks do not result in life ̄threatening ~~injurys~~ injuries or death.

WEEK 13: The Next Generation

■ **Using the Right Word, Subject-Verb Agreement, Comma (Series), Pronoun-Antecedent Agreement, Combining Sentences**

In Iraq, date-palm trees is a source of wealth. And it are passed down from one generation to the next. European families often passes down its jewelry or art. American families may save their fine furniture dishes and silverware for generations to come. No matter where families live, it seems, people enjoy giving they're children keepsakes from the past, and there heirs are grateful to receive these mementoes.

Corrected Paragraph

In Iraq, date-palm trees ~~is~~ *are* a source of wealth*,* ~~A~~*and* ~~it~~ *they* are passed down from one generation to the next. European families often ~~passes~~ *pass* down ~~its~~ *their* jewelry or art. American families may save their fine furniture*,* dishes*,* and silverware for generations to come. No matter where families live, it seems, people enjoy giving ~~they're~~ *their* children keepsakes from the past, and ~~there~~ *their* heirs are grateful to receive these mementoes.

WEEK 14: Live It Up!

■ **End Punctuation, Quotation Marks, Adjective (Comparative/Superlative), Verb (Tense), Abbreviations**

The life span of people is increasing in most countries of the world A girl born in 1994 in Japan or France can expect to live 82.3 years— until 2076! The European country of Georgia claims to have many people who are more than 110 yrs. old. What's the secret! When one old man was asked how he managed to live so long, he replies, I sleep with my hat on. That is probably not what helped him have a more long life span.

Corrected Paragraph

The life span of people is increasing in most countries of the world(.) A girl born in 1994 in Japan or France can expect to live 82.3 years— until 2076! The European country of Georgia claims to have many people who are more than 110 ~~yrs.~~ *years* old. What's the secret ?When one old man was asked how he managed to live so long, he ~~replies,~~ *replied* "I sleep with my hat on."That is probably not what helped him have a ~~more long~~ *longer* life span.

WEEK 15: Unsolved Mysteries

■ **Capitalization, Run-On Sentence, Using the Right Word, End Punctuation, Misplaced Modifier, Spelling**

Mysteries around the world raze questions about alien travelers from outer space. Today in the united states, a small percentage of UFO reports cannot be explained buy investigaters. Centuries ago in south america, someone made long gouges that resemble landing strips in the earth's surface. And in Ancient china, people built towns from the air that looked like animals. Were these people expecting visitors from the skies. Some say yes what do you think.

Corrected Paragraph

Mysteries around the world ~~raze~~ *raise* questions about alien travelers from outer space. Today in the ~~u~~nited ~~s~~tates, a small percentage of UFO reports cannot be explained ~~buy investigaters~~ *by investigators*. Centuries ago in ~~s~~outh ~~a~~merica, someone made long gouges that resemble landing strips in the earth's surface. And in Ancient ~~c~~hina, people built towns ~~from the air~~ that looked like animals *from the air*. Were these people expecting visitors from the skies~~.~~? Some say yes~~,~~ what do you think~~.~~?

WEEK 16: Three Firsts

■ **Numbers, Sentence Fragment, Verb (Irregular), Plurals, Adjective (Articles), Double Subject**

Take a look at these firsts! In 1927, Violet Cordery she becomed the first women to drive around the world, traveling 10,266 miles at twenty-four miles per hour. In 1993, Jim Abbott he was the first person, born without a right hand, to pitch a no-hitter in the major leagues. Isaac Murphy, a African American jockey, the first riders to win the Kentucky Derby 3 times. The next time someone tells you that you are the wrong sex, the wrong size, or a wrong anything, remember these facts. Then go for it!

Corrected Paragraph

Take a look at these firsts! In 1927, Violet Cordery ~~she~~ ~~becomed~~ *became* the first ~~women~~ *woman* to drive around the world, traveling 10,266 miles at ~~twenty-four~~ *24* miles per hour. In 1993, Jim Abbott ~~he~~ was the first person, born without a right hand, to pitch a no-hitter in the major leagues. Isaac Murphy, ~~a~~ *an* African American jockey, *became* the first ~~riders~~ *rider* to win the Kentucky Derby ~~3~~ *three* times. The next time someone tells you that you are the wrong sex, the wrong size, or ~~a~~ *the* wrong anything, remember these facts. Then go for it!

WEEK 17: Hoops

■ **Comma (Addresses and Nonrestrictive Phrases and Clauses), Spelling, Semicolon, Numbers, Verb (Tense), Subject-Verb Agreement**

Basketball was invented in Springfield Massachusetts and is become the world's most popular indoor sport. The Basketball Association of America and the National Basketball League merged in 1949 forming the National Basketball Association or NBA. The NBA is our country's largest profesional basketball leag. It consist of twenty-nine teams divided into two conferences and 4 divisions. Each of the 29 teams play an 82-game schedule in the regular season then the best teams competes in the championship play-offs.

Corrected Paragraph

Basketball was invented in Springfield, Massachusetts, and ~~is~~ *has* become the world's most popular indoor sport. The Basketball Association of America and the National Basketball League merged in 1949 forming the National Basketball Association, or NBA. The NBA is our country's largest ~~profesional~~ *professional* basketball ~~leag.~~ *league; consists* It ~~consist~~ of ~~twenty-nine~~ *29* teams divided into two conferences and *four* 4 divisions. Each of the 29 teams ~~play~~ *plays* an 82-game schedule in the regular season, then the best teams ~~competes~~ *compete* in the championship play-offs.

WEEK 18: Barreling Along

■ **Capitalization, Comma (Appositives), Pronoun-Antecedent Agreement, Comma Splice, Italics and Underlining**

Last summer my family and I saw niagara falls, we put on yellow raincoats and rode on a tour boat, maid of the mist, up the river below the falls. As the water thundered around them, the guide told them that Anna Taylor a daring schoolteacher was the first person ever to ride over Niagara Falls in a barrel. My stomach turned upside down as I imagined her plummeting over the edge. Then I thought of our own teacher going over the falls in a barrel, I laughed out loud.

Corrected Paragraph

Last summer my family and I saw ~~n~~iagara ~~f~~alls~~,~~ ~~w~~e put on yellow raincoats and rode on a tour boat, ~~m~~aid of the ~~m~~ist, up the river below the falls. As the water thundered around ~~them~~ us, the guide told ~~them~~ us that Anna Taylor, a daring schoolteacher, was the first person ever to ride over Niagara Falls in a barrel. My stomach turned upside down as I imagined her plummeting over the edge. Then I thought of ~~our~~ my own teacher going over the falls in a barrel, and I laughed out loud.

WEEK 19: Environmentally Friendly?

■ **Wordy Sentence, Comma (To Separate Phrases and Clauses), Dash,
Subject-Verb Agreement, Adjective (Articles)**

Which takes longer to totally break down and decay: a soda can or a glass bottle? While it take an aluminum metal soda can about 500 years to decay the ordinary glass bottle may remain unchanged and stay the same for a million years. Well, I guess that makes sense. I'm not surprised who ever heard of a genie in a soda can anyway?

Corrected Paragraph

Which takes longer to totally break down and decay: a soda can or a glass bottle? While it ~~take~~ *takes* an aluminum ~~metal~~ soda can about 500 years to decay, ~~the~~ *an* ordinary glass bottle may remain unchanged ~~and stay the same~~ for a million years. Well, I guess that makes sense. I'm not surprised—who ever heard of a genie in a soda can anyway?

WEEK 20: Toxic Trash

■ **Apostrophe (Possessives), Subject-Verb Agreement, Comma (Series), Combining Sentences, Abbreviations**

Although many industries safely disposes of their hazardous materials, some of Americas toxic waste are dumped illegally into fields ditches sewers and streams. Toxic dumping must stop now, because it pollutes rivers and lakes kills fish and water plants and destroys recreation areas. It can also endanger water supplies pollute the air or create a fire hazard. Not only people in the U.S., but people everywhere must protest such careless actions. People must demands responsible disposal of all toxic waste.

Corrected Paragraph

Although many industries safely ~~disposes~~ *dispose* of their hazardous materials, some of America's toxic waste ~~are~~ *is* dumped illegally into fields, ditches, sewers, and streams. Toxic dumping must stop now, because it pollutes rivers and lakes, kills fish and water plants, and destroys recreation areas. It can also endanger water supplies, pollute the air, or create a fire hazard. Not only people in the ~~U.S.~~ *United States*, but people everywhere must protest such careless actions, *and* ~~People~~ must ~~demands~~ *demand* responsible disposal of all toxic waste.

WEEK 21: A Great Lake, Again

■ **Comma (Appositives), Using the Right Word, Comma Splice,
Adjective (Comparative/Superlative), Abbreviations**

How do environmentalists clean up a lake? Lake Erie the fourth most largest of the Great Lakes was once declared dead by scientists because it was so polluted. A great number of fish had dyed, and swimming was unsafe. In 1972, the governments of Canada and the U.S. agreed to clean up the lake, today it is alive again. This major success story can serve as an example of how too restore other freshwater lakes who are in trouble.

Corrected Paragraph

How do environmentalists clean up a lake? Lake Erie ,the fourth most largest of the Great Lakes ,was once declared dead by scientists because it was so polluted. A great number of fish had ~~dyed~~ *died*, and swimming was unsafe. In 1972, the governments of Canada and the ~~U.S.~~ *United States* agreed to clean up the lake ,(or). today it is alive again. This major success story can serve as an example of how ~~too~~ *to* restore other freshwater lakes ~~who~~ *that* are in trouble.

WEEK 22: Women's Rights

- **Double Negative, Numbers, Using the Right Word, Period, Parallelism, Verb (Tense)**

In the colonies, most women weren't being allowed to go to school, didn't learn how to read, and couldn't never vote. In the eighteen hundreds, some girls learned reading, writing, and arithmetic in one-room schoolhouses. By 1900, some universities were educating women. In the early 1900s, Susan B Anthony lead the fight for women's voting rights. Change was slow sometimes, especially when it replaces opinions held for centuries.

Corrected Paragraph

In the colonies, most women weren't ~~being~~ allowed to go to school, didn't learn how to read, and couldn't ~~never~~ vote. In the ~~eighteen hundreds~~ *1800s*, some girls learned reading, writing, and arithmetic in one-room schoolhouses. By 1900, some universities were educating women. In the early 1900s, Susan B̶.̶Anthony ~~lead~~ *led* the fight for women's voting rights. Change ~~was~~ *is* slow sometimes, especially when it replaces opinions held for centuries.

WEEK 23: Forever Free

■ Numbers, Verb (Irregular), Sentence Fragment, Nonstandard Language, Spelling, Comma (Dates)

200 years ago, the original Declaration of Independence would of freed all the slaves; but Thomas Jefferson bowed to pressure from other delegates and taken that part out. As a result, slavery continyued for almost one hundred years until January 1 1863. On that day, President Abraham Lincoln delivered the Emancipation Proclamation. To set all persons of the United States "thenceforeword, and forever free." For this, Lincoln knowed as the "Great Emancipator."

Corrected Paragraph

Two hundred
~~200~~ years ago, the original Declaration of Independence would ~~of~~ *have*

freed all the slaves; but Thomas Jefferson bowed to pressure from other

delegates and ~~taken~~ *took* that part out. As a result, slavery ~~continyued~~ *continued* for

almost ~~one hundred~~ *100* years until January 1 ̂, 1863. On that day, President

Abraham Lincoln delivered the Emancipation Proclamation ̸ ̸To set all *t*

persons of the United States "thenceforeword, and forever free." For this,

is known
Lincoln ̂ ~~knowed~~ as the "Great Emancipator."

WEEK 24: The Weekly Bath

■ Comma (Unnecessary and To Separate Phrases and Clauses), Dash,
Adjective (Comparative/Superlative), Using the Right Word,
Subject-Verb Agreement

In the 1800s, it were common for people to take baths only once a week. First the water had to be hauled into the house no easy task from the well or stream! Then some of it had to be heated, on a wood-burning stove and added gradually to the more cooler water in the tub who was often located in the kitchen. In many homes, the hole family tooks turns sharing the bathwater. Imagine waiting for you're turn, in a family of eight!

Corrected Paragraph

In the 1800s, it ~~were~~ *was* common for people to take baths only once a week. First the water had to be hauled into the house⎯ no easy task⎯ from the well or stream! Then some of it had to be heated, on a wood-burning stove and added gradually to the ~~more~~ cooler water in the tub, *which* ~~who~~ was often located in the kitchen. In many homes, the ~~hole~~ *whole* family *took* ~~tooks~~ turns sharing the bathwater. Imagine waiting for *your* ~~you're~~ turn, in a family of eight!

WEEK 25: The Cost of War

■ **Capitalization, Numbers, Using the Right Word, Plurals, Verb (Irregular), Comma (To Separate Phrases and Clauses)**

War touches more lifes than statistics tell. The american civil war, fighted between eighteen sixty one and 1865, caused six-hundred and twenty thousand casualties. Even after the war the devastation continued to effect many more people. When fathers and sons dyed in battle there families were left without much help to rebuild they're war-ravaged homes and businesss. Some people never recovered from the emotional and economic wounds; the war changed their lifes forever.

Corrected Paragraph

War touches more ~~lifes~~ *lives* than statistics tell. The *A*merican *c*ivil *w*ar, ~~fighted~~ *fought* between ~~eighteen sixty one~~ *1861* and 1865, caused ~~six-hundred and twenty thousand~~ *620,000* casualties. Even after the war*,* the devastation continued to ~~effect~~ *affect* many more people. When fathers and sons ~~dyed~~ *died* in battle*,* ~~there~~ *their* families were left without much help to rebuild ~~they're~~ *their* war-ravaged homes and ~~businesss~~ *businesses.* Some people never recovered from the emotional and economic wounds; the war changed their ~~lifes~~ *lives* forever.

WEEK 26: Peacemaker Assassinated

■ **Comma (Dates, To Enclose Information, and To Separate Phrases and Clauses), Using the Right Word, Capitalization, Spelling**

Martin Luther king jr. won the Nobel Piece Prize in 1964 for leading nonviolent, Civil-Rights protests. Despite his call for peaceful activism entire cities were scenes of mass riots and violance during the early '60s. For years people protested against poverty—a major problem in the central cities. The number of crimes such as murder and robbery sored. King himself fell to an assassin's bullet on April 4 1968.

Corrected Paragraph

Martin Luther King, Jr., won the Nobel ~~Piece~~ *Peace* Prize in 1964 for leading nonviolent, Civil-Rights protests. Despite his call for peaceful activism, entire cities were scenes of mass riots and ~~violance~~ *violence* during the early '60s. For years, people protested against poverty—a major problem in the central cities. The number of crimes such as murder and robbery ~~sored~~ *soared*. King himself fell to an assassin's bullet on April 4, 1968.

WEEK 27: Seeing Is Believing?

■ **Adjective (Comparative/Superlative), Subject-Verb Agreement, Quotation Marks, Comma (Dialogue and Direct Address)**

My mom always says Tanya believe nothing of what you hear and only half of what you see. She says I'll understand this saying as I get more older, but I understand it now. For example, when Mom says my room need cleaning, I doesn't believe her. I know my room are only half as messy as it look! After all, my most best friend's room look twice as messy as mine do.

Corrected Paragraph

My mom always says, "Tanya, believe nothing of what you hear and only half of what you see." She says I'll understand this saying as I get ~~more~~ older, but I understand it now. For example, when Mom says my room *needs* ~~need~~ cleaning, I *don't* ~~doesn't~~ believe her. I know my room *is* ~~are~~ only half as messy as it *looks* ~~look~~! After all, my ~~most~~ best friend's room *looks* ~~look~~ twice as messy as mine *does* ~~do~~.

WEEK 28: Early to Bed

■ **Comma (Series), Quotation Marks, Double Negative, Verb (Tense), Adjective (Articles), Double Subject**

Benjamin Franklin he accomplished a great deal in many fields: he is a inventor a civic leader a writer a printer a publisher a scientist and a gardener. He was born in Boston, Massachusetts, in 1706 but run away to Philadelphia, Pennsylvania, at age 17, and there he live until his death in 1790. In his long and useful life, he must not never have forgetted the advice he writes in *Poor Richard's Almanac*: Early to bed and early to rise makes a man healthy, wealthy, and wise.

Corrected Paragraph

Benjamin Franklin ~~he~~ accomplished a great deal in many fields: he ~~is~~ *was* *an* ~~a~~ inventor, a civic leader, a writer, a printer, a publisher, a scientist, and a gardener. He was born in Boston, Massachusetts, in 1706 but ~~run~~ *ran* away to Philadelphia, Pennsylvania, at age 17, and there he ~~live~~ *lived* until his death in 1790. In his long and useful life, he must ~~not~~ never have ~~forgetted~~ *forgotten* the advice he ~~writes~~ *wrote* in *Poor Richard's Almanac*: "Early to bed and early to rise makes a man healthy, wealthy, and wise."

WEEK 29: The Islamic Religion

■ **Subject-Verb Agreement, Comma (Appositives), Using the Right Word, Semicolon, Comma Splice**

One of the most widely practiced religions of the Western world are Islam. Founded in Arabia during the seventh century by Muhammad an Arab preacher Islam grew quickly. Muhammad believed that he were God's messenger, his companions preserved his teachings in the Koran the holy book of Islam. By around 750 C.E., one-third of the people in the world had excepted the Islamic faith, they were called Muslims. Islam still unite millions of people, they represent a variety of cultures all over the world today.

Corrected Paragraph

One of the most widely practiced religions of the Western world ~~are~~ *is* Islam. Founded in Arabia during the seventh century by Muhammad ,an Arab preacher ,Islam grew quickly. Muhammad believed that he ~~were~~ *was* God's messenger. His companions preserved his teachings in the Koran ,the holy book of Islam. By around 750 C.E., one-third of the people in the world had ~~excepted~~ *accepted* the Islamic faith ; they were called Muslims. Islam still ~~unite~~ *unites* millions of people ; they represent a variety of cultures all over the world today.

WEEK 30: So Long

■ **Verb (Irregular), Hyphen (Single-Thought Adjectives), Using the Right Word, Pronoun (Reflexive), End Punctuation, Capitalization**

Have you ever planned a trip for you and your family. It's a good idea to make a list of items to took along. It's so easy too overpack, especially for an extended journey. The famous traveler marco Polo, an italian trader, taked a 24 year trip to china in the late 1200s. Do you think he new he'd be gone that long. How many peaces of luggage do you think he taken along?

Corrected Paragraph

Have you ever planned a trip for ~~you~~ *yourself* and your family*?* It's a good idea to make a list of items to ~~took~~ *take* along. It's so easy ~~too~~ *to* overpack, especially for an extended journey. The famous traveler *M*arco Polo, an *I*talian trader, ~~taked~~ *took* a 24*-*year trip to *C*hina in the late 1200s. Do you think he ~~new~~ *knew* he'd be gone that long*?* How many ~~peaces~~ *pieces* of luggage do you think he ~~taken~~ *took* along?

WEEK 31: Being in Fashion

■ **Using the Right Word, Plurals, Comma (To Separate Phrases and Clauses), Colon, Capitalization, Subject-Verb Agreement, Interjection**

Fashion customs from the passed seems outlandish to us today. For example in Medieval Japan fashionable women dyed their teeth black. Yuck. In nineteenth-century America refined ladys had their lower ribs broken in order to make there waistlines smaller. Ouch. Consider the fashion trends of today body-piercing, studs, tattoos. Which ones will seem strange to people 50 years from now?

Corrected Paragraph

Fashion customs from the ~~passed~~ *past* ~~seems~~ *seem* outlandish to us today. For example‚ in *M*edieval Japan fashionable women dyed their teeth black. Yuck‚! In nineteenth-century America‚ refined ~~ladys~~ *ladies* had their lower ribs broken in order to make ~~there~~ *their* waistlines smaller. Ouch‚! Consider the fashion trends of today‚ body-piercing, studs, tattoos. Which ones will seem strange to people 50 years from now?

WEEK 32: Human Longevity

■ **Comma (To Separate Phrases and Clauses), Using the Right Word, Verb (Tense), Spelling**

In the sixteenth century the average person lives to be 35 years old. That's not very old. Obviusly, people has to grow up faster, marry younger, and have children earlier then today. Probably not very many people became grandparents. Today, thousands of people live to reach 100, and they become great-great-great-grandparents. That's alot of grandchildren!

Corrected Paragraph

In the sixteenth century, the average person ~~lives~~ *lived* to be 35 years old. That's not very old. ~~Obviusly,~~ *Obviously* people ~~has~~ *had* to grow up faster, marry younger, and have children earlier ~~then~~ *than* today. Probably not very many people became grandparents. Today, thousands of people live to reach 100, and they become great-great-great-grandparents. That's ~~alot~~ *a lot* of grandchildren!

WEEK 33: The First Step

■ **Hyphen (Single-Thought Adjectives), Subject-Verb Agreement, Numbers, Rambling Sentence**

They say that all journeys begins with the first step, and sometimes they end that way instead because my grandmother was only a child when she traveled from Europe to America with her family in 1906, and like millions of others around the world, her family had left their well loved home to start a new life. Barely beginning to walk, my 1 year old grandmother took her first steps on American soil.

Corrected Paragraph

They say that all journeys ~~begins~~ *begin* with the first step. and sometimes *S*ometimes they end that way instead. ~~because~~ *M*y grandmother was only a child when she traveled from Europe to America with her family in 1906. and *L*ike millions of others around the world, her family had left their well- loved home to start a new life. Barely beginning to walk, my ~~1~~ *one*-year-old grandmother took her first steps on American soil.

Did I make

WEEK 34: Snow Joke

■ **Subject-Verb Agreement, Using the Right Word, Capitalization, Colon or Dash, Wordy Sentence**

Did you know that eskimos have more than 20 different words that mean "snow" in their language? Its not surprising. In they're frozen climate where it is cold so much of the year, their lives and livelihoods depends on understanding and knowing a lot about the whether. Their are many words in english with basically the same meaning. Too find them, use a thesaurus a reference book that lists thousands of words and there synonyms.

Corrected Paragraph

Did you know that *E*skimos have more than 20 different words that mean "snow" in their language? ~~Its~~ *It's* not surprising. In ~~they're~~ *their* frozen climate ~~where it is cold so much of the year,~~ their lives and livelihoods ~~depends~~ *depend* on understanding ~~and knowing a lot about~~ the ~~whether.~~ *weather.* ~~Their~~ *There* are many words in *E*nglish with basically the same meaning. ~~Too~~ *To* find them, use a thesaurus *(or)—* , a reference book that lists thousands of words and ~~there~~ *their* synonyms.

WEEK 35: Say the Word

■ **Comma (Numbers and Interjections), Verb (Irregular), Run-On Sentence, Pronoun-Antecedent Agreement**

English is the most widely spoken language in the world it has more active words—about 500000—than any other known language. With a half-million words to chose from, why would anyone rely on the same few? Well if people learned just two new words each day, they'd add about 7300 words to my vocabulary in 10 years.

Corrected Paragraph

English is the most widely spoken language in the world. It has more
active words—about 500,000—than any other known language. With a
choose
half-million words to ~~chose~~ from, why would anyone rely on the same
few? Well, if people learned just two new words each day, they'd add about
their
7,300 words to ~~my~~ vocabulary in 10 years.

improve
punctuate

Daily Writing Practice

This section offers three types of exercises. **Writing prompts** are sentences and pictures designed to inspire freewriting (which students may share in class and later shape into finished narratives or essays). **Writing topics** address a wide range of writing ideas. Finally, the **Show-Me sentences** provide practice in developing the important skill of "showing" in writing.

SPELL edit
capitalize

Writing Prompts

A Writing Prompts FAQ Sheet

You may duplicate the following question-and-answer information about writing prompts as a handout for students or as the basis for a class discussion.

Anyone who wants to be a good writer has to practice often. That's why so many writers keep journals and diaries. And that's why your teacher asks you to write something nearly every day in school. Your teacher may ask you to write about a specific topic or about a personal experience. Your teacher might also ask you to use a writing prompt.

A writing prompt can be anything from a question to a photograph to a quotation. The idea is for you to write whatever you can without planning or researching the topic. You simply write what you have inside. And you keep writing until all your thoughts are gone. That's it!

How do I get started? It's really very simple. You just write down whatever comes into your mind when you think about your writing prompt. This doesn't have to be much. All you are looking for is an idea to get you going.

Shouldn't I plan out what I'm going to write about? No, you shouldn't plan anything. That's the whole idea. Just write. You don't need to know where your writing will take you. Mystery is good; in fact, it is the mystery and surprises along the way that get writers hooked on writing.

What can I do to keep my writing going? Don't stop! When you run out of ideas, shift gears and try writing about your topic in a slightly different way. For example, you might compare your topic to something else. Or you might invent dialogue between two or more people who are discussing your topic. Or you might think of a specific audience—like a group of first graders—and write so they can understand your topic. Whatever you do, keep the ideas flowing as freely as possible.

When should I stop? If you are doing a timed writing (3, 5, or 10 minutes), stop when the time is up. Otherwise, you might decide it's time to stop when you've filled up the entire page. (Or you might keep going, using another sheet of paper.) Or you might decide to stop when you feel that you've done as much thinking and writing as you can and your brain is drained.

What do I do with my writing? You might share it with a classmate and see what she or he thinks. Or you might turn your writing into a more polished essay, story, or poem. Or you might set it aside and use it later when you need a topic for a writing assignment.

So, really, all I have to do is just start writing? Right!

WRITING PROMPT

When I saw . . .

_____

_____

_____

_____

_____

_____

_____

_____

_____

_____

_____

_____

_____

_____

_____

_____

_____

_____

WRITING PROMPT

Everyone was in a panic!

WRITING PROMPT

Touchdown! We made it!

_____

_____

_____

_____

_____

_____

_____

_____

_____

_____

WRITING PROMPT

It was the greatest ride!

_____

_____

_____

_____

_____

_____

_____

_____

_____

_____

_____

_____

_____

_____

_____

_____

WRITING PROMPT
The perfect place to live...

WRITING PROMPT

There was always something strange about that house . . .

_____

_____

_____

_____

_____

_____

_____

_____

_____

_____

_____

_____

_____

_____

_____

_____

_____

124

WRITING PROMPT

That's one problem we HAVE to solve!

WRITING PROMPT
Music!

DESTINO

WRITING PROMPT (Write your own.)

WRITING PROMPT

When I get older . . .

_____

_____

_____

_____

_____

_____

_____

_____

_____

_____

_____

_____

_____

_____

_____

_____

_____

_____

WRITING PROMPT

If machines could think . . .

WRITING PROMPT

The next thing I knew...

_____

_____

_____

_____

_____

_____

_____

_____

_____

_____

_____

_____

_____

_____

_____

_____

_____

_____

WRITING PROMPT

Pets

_____

_____

_____

_____

_____

_____

_____

_____

_____

_____

_____

_____

_____

_____

_____

_____

WRITING PROMPT

Creepy, crawly things!

_____

_____

_____

_____

_____

_____

_____

_____

_____

_____

_____

_____

_____

_____

_____

_____

_____

WRITING PROMPT (Draw your own.)

WRITING PROMPT

The only sound in the night air . . .

_____

_____

_____

_____

_____

_____

_____

_____

_____

_____

_____

_____

_____

_____

_____

_____

_____

WRITING PROMPT

Money can't buy . . .

_____

_____

_____

_____

_____

_____

_____

_____

_____

_____

_____

_____

_____

_____

_____

_____

WRITING PROMPT

First Flight

Writing Topics

Daily Journal Writing

"I can tap into [my students'] human instincts to write if I help them realize that their lives and memories are worth telling stories about, and if I help them zoom in on topics of fundamental importance to them."

—writing teacher June Gould

As classroom teachers, we know from firsthand experience that the personal stories young learners love to share can serve as the basis of an effective and lively writing program. Here's how we did it:

Getting Started

At the beginning of the school year, we introduced in-class journal writing to the students. (We encouraged students to write outside of class in journals as well, but the journals in school were part of our writing program.) We knew that the most effective way to get students into writing was simply to let them write often and freely about their own lives, without having to worry about grades or turning their writing in. This helped them develop a feel for "real" writing—writing that originates from their own thoughts and feelings.

That's where the journals come in. Nothing gets a student into writing more effectively than a personal journal. (And no other type of writing is so easy to implement.) All your students need are spiral notebooks, pens, time to write, and encouragement to explore whatever is on their minds. (See pages 431–434 in *Write Source* for more information.)

We provided our students with four or five personal writing topics each time they wrote. They could use one of these topics as a starting point, or write about something else entirely. The choice was theirs. (We found that providing writing topics was much easier and more productive than going into our "You've got plenty to write about" song and dance.)

Writing Topics

To start off an exercise, we posted a list of suggested writing topics like these:

- your most memorable kitchen-related experience,
- coping with younger brothers or sisters,
- being home alone, late at night, or
- what you did over the past weekend.

Students would either choose from the list or write about a topic they preferred. See pages 141–144 for more suggested topics.

We asked our students to write every other day for the first 10 minutes of the class period. (Monday, Wednesday, and Friday were writing days.) Of course, we had to adjust our schedule at times, but, for the most part, students wrote three times a week.

Keeping It Going

After everyone was seated and roll was taken, the journals were passed out, the topics were given, and everyone wrote. We expected students to write for a full 10 minutes, nonstop. And we made sure that they did. They knew that they would earn a quarterly journal grade based on the number of words they produced. This almost made a contest out of the writing sessions. Each time they wrote, they wanted to see if they could increase their production from past journal entries, and they always wanted to write more than their classmates.

> "Over the last fifteen years, a number of teachers around the country and their students have been amazed by what happened when people write ten to fifteen minutes without worrying about grammar, spelling, or punctuation, and concentrating only on telling some kind of truth."
>
> —Ken Macrorie

Wrapping It Up

On days that we weren't writing, we shared journal entries. First, each student exchanged journals with a classmate. He or she would count the number of words in the latest entry, read it carefully, and then make comments on things he or she liked or questioned. After each pair had shared their comments with one another, we talked about the entries as a class.

Many writers were reluctant to share their entries with the entire group. But the readers had no problem volunteering someone else's entry ("You've got to hear Nick's story") and reading it out loud. The students loved these readings and the discussions that followed.

Personal Experience Papers

Periodically, we would interrupt the normal course of journal writing and make formal writing assignments. That is, we would ask students to review their entries and select one (or part of one) to develop into a more polished, complete personal experience paper. Usually, those entries that readers had enjoyed and wanted to know more about would be the ones the young writers chose to develop.

We wanted to make sure that their writing went through at least one or two thorough revisions, so we gave our writers plenty of class time to work on their papers. We also required them to turn in all preliminary work with their final drafts. (See pages 97–134 in *Write Source* for guidelines for this type of writing.)

The experience papers were shared with the entire class at the end of the project. This was a fun and informal activity, but one that students came to appreciate as an important part of the entire composing process. It was their day. They were on stage. They were sharing the culmination of all their hard work—a special moment in their own lives.

Writing Topics

The topics on the following pages can be used as daily writing prompts for journal or personal writing.

Definitions

- Courage is . . .
- Happiness is . . .
- Music is . . .
- A pet is . . .
- A friend is . . .
- Having fun is . . .
- A good teacher is . . .
- Summer is . . .
- Loneliness is . . .

Characterization

- If I were . . .
- If I were principal . . .
- If I were old . . .
- If I were lost . . .
- If I were famous . . .
- If I were deaf . . .

Other Times and Places

- If I could . . .
- If I could be anyone . . .
- If I could relive yesterday . . .
- If I could live in a different time period . . .
- If I could have one wish . . .
- If I could make three wishes . . .
- If I could design my very own town, I would . . .
- If I could give any gift in the world, I would . . .

Titles

- The Broken Computer
- The Blob That Ate (my city)
- The Money Tree
- The Magic Door
- The Flat Tire
- The Missing Shoe
- The Day the Music Died
- Instant Celebrity

Writing Topics

Best and Worst, First and Last

- My craziest experience in a restaurant or shopping mall

- An unforgettable dream

- My first bicycle

- My pet's strange habits

- My father or mother made a mistake!

- A special place

- What makes a best friend?

- A race I've been in

- Fake illnesses I've "suffered" from

- My saddest memory

Stepping Out

- The most fun I've had recently

- My biggest surprise

- Music and me

- Stings, scrapes, and burns

- I get great joy out of the dumbest things.

As My World Turns

- A visit to a relative's house

- Summer vacation means . . .

- Places to visit in my city or county

- The worst things to wait for

- Guess what I just heard!

- I jumped for joy when I heard the good news.

- What I saw on the way home from school yesterday

- Why am I always being compared to _____ ?

- What is important to me?

Mixed Bag

- Who sets a good example?

- It all started with . . .

- Don't throw that away!

- Which is better: a good book or a good movie?

- Life as an identical twin

Writing Topics

School Talk

- Dear Blackboard,

- My first school memories

- What makes school exciting?

- The first day of school is the worst/best.

All About Me

- Things I like and why

- My favorite movie

- Silly things I've done

- The most "frightening" thing to me

- What embarrasses me the most?

- When do I feel the happiest?

- Just leave me alone.

- When I get mad, I . . .

- In January 2020, I'll be . . .

- Being lazy didn't pay off when . . .

- The most unusual person I know

- I didn't mean to do it.

- Why did it have to be me?

- Was I sick!

I wonder . . .

- I wonder what it would be like to be blind.

- What will I be like as a senior citizen?

- I don't understand why . . .

- I wonder why . . .

Science Fiction and Tall Tales

- The time machine

- Tiny people invade the classroom.

- The adventure of the red knight

- The last encounter

- Hot-air escape

- The lost contact lens

- The haunted cabin

- The mystery of Sam Stone

- The last telephone call

- Suddenly the rope snapped!

- I slowly lifted the lid and . . .

Writing Topics

Compare and Contrast

- Freshwater to salt water
- Snow skiing to waterskiing
- Radio to television
- An amusement park to a nature preserve
- A river to a highway
- Outdoor jobs to desk jobs
- Talking by phone to communicating via e-mail
- Regular cooking to microwave cooking
- Name brands to generics
- Wilderness frontiers to undersea frontiers
- Outer space to ocean depths
- Regular farming to dryland farming
- Regular foods to hydroponic foods

Real-Life Happenings

- My bravest moment
- My funniest experience
- The scariest time
- My worst meal
- My hero
- The oddest thing
- My longest trip
- My greatest adventure
- The biggest mix-up
- An embarrassing moment
- A favorite relative
- My worst haircut
- My best birthday

Show-Me Sentences

Producing Writing with Detail

From time immemorial, teachers have said to their students, "Your essay lacks details" or "This idea is too general" or "Show, don't tell." We even know of a teacher who had a special stamp made: "Give more examples."

So how should this writing problem be approached? It's obvious that simply telling students to add more details and examples is not enough. Even showing them how professional writers develop their ideas is not enough (although this does help). Students learn to add substance and depth to their writing through regular practice.

Here's one method that has worked for many students and teachers: *Show-Me* sentences. Students begin with a basic topic— "My locker is messy," for example—and create a paragraph or brief essay that *shows* rather than *tells*. The sentence is a springboard for lively writing.

About Your Show-Me Sentences

The following pages contain 45 Show-Me sentences. Each sentence speaks directly to middle-school students, so they should have little difficulty creating essays full of personal details. Again, we suggest that you use these sentences every other day for an extended period of time (at least a month).

Note: By design, each page of Show-Me sentences can be made into an overhead transparency.

Implementation

DAY ONE Before you ask students to work on their own, develop a Show-Me sentence as a class. Start by writing a sample sentence on the board. Then have students volunteer specific details that give this basic thought some life. List their ideas on the board. Next, construct a brief paragraph on the board using some of these details. (Make no mention of the original sentence in your paragraph.) Discuss the results. Make sure that your students see how specific details help create a visual image for the reader. Also have your students read and react to examples of "showing writing" from professional texts. (Share the model on page 147 with your students.)

DAY TWO Have students work on their first Show-Me sentences in class. Upon completion of their writing, have pairs of students share the results of their work. Then ask for volunteers to share their writing with the entire class. (Make copies of strong writing for future class discussions.)

DAY THREE Ask students to develop a new paragraph. At the beginning of the *next* class period, discuss the results (break into pairs as before). Continue in this fashion for at least a month.

Note: Reserve the first 10 or 15 minutes of each class period for writing or discussing. (Students who don't finish their writing in class should have it ready for the next day.)

Evaluation

Students should reserve a section in their notebooks for their writing or compile their work in a folder. At regular intervals, give them some type of performance score for their efforts. At the end of the unit, have them select one or two of their best examples to revise and submit for a thorough evaluation.

Enrichment

This method of instruction is based on the work of writing instructor Rebekah Caplan. She has developed an extensive program to help students produce well-detailed, engaging essays through regular practice. She makes the following suggestions:

● Have your students turn cliches like *It's a small world* or *Accidents will happen* into strong narrative or descriptive paragraphs.

● Have them develop sentences like *Friday nights are better than Saturday nights* into paragraphs that compare and contrast two subjects.

● In addition, have students convert loaded statements like *Noon hours are too short* or *I don't need a curfew* into opinion pieces.

Note: In a sense, these variations become progressively more challenging. Most student writers, for example, have more difficulty supporting an opinion than they have illustrating the basic ideas behind a cliche.

● You might also use vocabulary words in Show-Me sentences or connect these sentences to literary works under study. (Generally speaking, Show-Me sentences can be linked to any unit of study.)

Sample Writing

My baby sister was the picture of health.
(telling sentence)

Josie flitted from one thing to another, as if everything in the kitchen were there for her amusement. She had already left a trail of pots, pans, bananas, and crackers behind her. Flashing Mom a bright-eyed smile, she reached her dimpled hands toward her juice cup. The juice dribbled down her chin as she drank. A swipe across her plump cheeks with her hand took care of that. She plunked the half-empty cup on the counter and started to sing to herself as she marched around the kitchen table. A sound from the yard suddenly caught her attention, and she ran toward the back door on eager little legs.

SHOW-ME SENTENCES

I've never been so cold.

I wouldn't want to be in his/her shoes.

It was an incredible sight to see!

The crowd went crazy!

It was the best book I've ever read.

SHOW-ME SENTENCES

It isn't always easy being a good friend.

The _____ really hit the spot.

It was the greatest _____ ever built by kids.

Learning to _____ isn't that easy.

Our _____ was a real disappointment.

SHOW-ME SENTENCES

We played it almost every night last summer.

Picking apples/berries can actually be fun.

Our neighborhood is always _____.

Nothing is better than _____ when you're really hungry.

My favorite comic strip is _____.

SHOW-ME SENTENCES

I still remember my _____.

The view from there was amazing.

Our kitchen is a real _____ in the morning.

It was the first _____ I ever attended.

They're the best music group around.

SHOW-ME SENTENCES

I wish I had a(n) _____.

It was so strange that I couldn't stop staring.

Our class is _____.

It was the greatest celebration I've ever attended.

My grandmother/grandfather is like nobody else I know.

SHOW-ME SENTENCES

_____ is my favorite TV show.

It was the worst/best time I've ever had.

Riding the bus is _____.

_____ is the best season of the year.

_____ deserves an award.

SHOW-ME SENTENCES

_____ would be the perfect job.

Animals can teach humans a lesson or two.

Some students really "add" to a class.

I felt really sick.

Sometimes he/she seems so _____.

SHOW-ME SENTENCES

The dog must have been lost.

He/She/It looked bigger in real life.

It was the noisiest thing I'd ever heard.

It was a real mess.

The clown was a bit unusual.

SHOW-ME SENTENCES

I wasn't even afraid.

It was the best advice I'd ever gotten.

Dreams can come true.

Telling the truth can be good/bad.

Everything turned out okay in the end.